The Novels
of Chinua Achebe

In series with this book
Protest & Conflict
in African Literature
edited by Cosmo Pieterse & Donald Munro

The Novels
of Chinua Achebe

G. D. KILLAM

Associate Professor of English
York University, Toronto

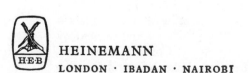

HEINEMANN
LONDON · IBADAN · NAIROBI

Heinemann Educational Books
48 Charles Street, London, WIX 8AH
POB 25080, Nairobi · PMB 5205, Ibadan
EDINBURGH MELBOURNE TORONTO
AUCKLAND HONG KONG SINGAPORE

SBN 435 18500 4 (hardback)
SBN 435 18501 4 (paperback)

Permission to quote from
Things Fall Apart and *No Longer at Ease*
is gratefully acknowledged
to William Heinemann, Ltd and Astor Honor Inc.
and from *Arrow of God* and *Man of the People*
to William Heinemann, Ltd and John Day Co. Inc.

Set in Monotype Plantin
and printed by
Cox & Wyman Ltd,
London, Fakenham and Reading

Contents

This book
is dedicated to
my Mother, Father
& Uncle

Introduction

▼▼▼▼▼▼▼▼▼▼▼▼▼▼▼▼▼▼▼▼▼▼▼▼▼▼▼▼▼▼

CHINUA ACHEBE is Nigeria's best-known novelist
and probably the best-known writer of fiction from black
Africa. He has written four novels which are widely read
in Africa and are now achieving an audience in Europe and North
America. Achebe attracted considerable attention when the publication of his fourth book, *A Man of the People* – the closing scenes
of which describe a military take-over from a corrupt civil régime
in a West African country – coincided with the first military coup
in Nigeria in January 1966. His reputation rests principally on his
first novel, *Things Fall Apart*, published in 1958, the first novel by
a Nigerian writer to have serious claim to consideration as literature. The novels which follow, *No Longer at Ease*, *Arrow of God*
and *A Man of the People* reveal no less certainly the serious approach
Achebe takes to the craft of fiction.

So much has been written about the anthropological and sociological significance of *Things Fall Apart* and *Arrow of God* – their
evocation of traditional nineteenth- and earlier twentieth-century
Ibo village life – so much about Achebe's attempt to write stories
which have the components of Aristotelian tragedy, that the overall
excellence of these books as pieces of fiction, as works of art has
been obscured. Similarly, the other novels with their modern
settings have been seen as Achebe's analysis of the conflicting
forces, political and social, which determine the quality of contemporary Nigerian life, and the focus of critical attention paid
these aspects of the books has meant that scant attention has been
paid them as works of literature.

Achebe recognizes that the societies he evokes in his books will
be generally unfamiliar to overseas readers. However carefully he
subordinates the background to the human life the novels create,
it is the former element which will likely attract attention. And this

is not without importance. These novels bring news of a strange part of the world and of the values and attitudes of a group of people who have only recently achieved prominence in world affairs. Modern African writing in one sense assists the decolonization process of peoples who have suffered the trauma of foreign conquest and the imposition of an alien culture. The appeal in this direction of a writer's work, especially a writer in modern Africa, is likely to be more local than general; but overseas readers have praised this aspect of Achebe's work. In this respect, as an interpreter of the cultural worth of his society, Achebe is no different than other writers in other places and times. Like them his claim to being a novelist in the fullest sense of the word does not rest on his success within this limited area of the novelist's function.

More recent comment on Achebe has sought to relate him to the literary traditions of England.[1] This is appropriate since not only does he write in English and prefer to be judged by the general critical standards which apply, but also he admits that the writers who have influenced him number among them Conrad, Graham Greene, Waugh and others, and thus it would be expected that his work would fit into the general pattern of English fiction in the twentieth century. To suggest the general literary milieu into which Achebe's work may be placed is to suggest a critical context for examining his work. It does not, however, account for the excellence of the writing.

Achebe has stated in a number of places his recognition of the unique situation in which the modern African writer finds himself. His prose writing offers explicit comment on the inheritance that both the writer and his society received from the colonial period and makes clear his views on a variety of related subjects, views which are offered implicitly in the fiction. His novels form a sequence and reflect, broadly speaking, the changes which have taken place in Ibo, and by implication Nigerian life as a result of what Achebe calls the 'chance encounter' between Europe and Africa during the imperial-colonial period. The prose writing reveals the same realistic appraisal, the same balance and objectivity as are found in the novels.

The modern African novel, of which to date Achebe is the major exponent, is similar to and yet different from fiction written within the established traditions of novel writing in English. It follows the main historical development of the English novel and it makes an addition of its own to that development. Similarities between the English literary tradition and that which is in its initial stage in Africa arise, principally, out of the fact that African writers have adopted the various novel forms from English and, more important, from the fact that the generality of them have adopted English or French – that is a world language – to encompass their African experience and inspiration. In accepting a world language as a medium of literary exchange, African novelists suggest a criteria by which they would wish their work to be judged. Differences between the established and the emerging traditions are more apparent and more salutary. These result not solely from innate racial differences, although ethnic considerations provide important thematic material in modern African writing. They stem rather from a group past with its ambiguous and generally bitter experience of colonialism, and from a group present which seeks to define the relevance of the colonial experience to the present. They stem further from the contact, in some cases collision, both historical and immediate, between the traditional folk and/or mythic pasts of various ethnic groups and their systems and values, and those imported from Europe. They result from a relatively brief nevertheless intense experience with separate and dominating institutions – political, social, educational and cultural – and express a desire to modify these to suit local and national needs by incorporating what is valuable in the colonial legacy whilst retaining an African identity. Modern African writing has been concerned exclusively with the reality of African life and no African writer of English expression to date has sought his thematic material outside Africa. Unlike writers in some countries with similar colonial pasts, African writers have not turned their backs on their own cultures; rather they have faced up to the problems and sought solutions for them in imaginative form. Their fiction is a literary echo of a general cultural reality.

Achebe is in the front rank of these writers and his prose writing reflects three essential and related concerns – first, with the legacy of colonialism at both the individual and societal level; secondly, with the *fact* of English as a language of national and international exchange; thirdly, with the obligations and responsibilities of the writer both to the society in which he lives and to his art. Achebe's

prose is worth attending to not only because it illuminates the
subject matter and method of his novels, but because it offers,
when considered with the fiction, an assessment of and an apology
(in the best sense of that word) for his adoption of a world language, his choice of subject matter and his obligations as an African
to his culture and his craft.

The following passages, extrapolated from various of Achebe's
prose writings, reveal not only his concern over the issues men-
tioned above but reveal, by the objectivity and disinterestedness of
his approach, his attempt to provide a rationale which not only
accounts for the historical reasons which have shaped the values
of modern African nations and their writers, but also suggests the
direction in which both might travel. Asking 'what are the factors
which conspired to place English in the position of a national
language in many parts of Africa?' and taking Nigeria as his example, Achebe writes:

> . . . these nations were created in the first place by the inter-
> vention of the British which, I hasten to add, is not saying that
> the peoples comprising these nations were invented by the
> British. . . . And I believe that in political and economic terms
> . . . this arbitrary creation called Nigeria holds out wonderful
> prospects. Yet the fact remains that Nigeria was created by the
> British – for their own ends. Let us give the devil his due:
> Colonialism in Africa disrupted many things, but it did create
> big political units where there were small scattered ones
> before. . . . Of course there are areas of Africa where colonialism
> divided a single ethnic group among two or even three powers.
> But on the whole it did bring together many peoples that had
> hitherto gone their several ways.[2]

In another place he reveals the moderateness of his views:

> I am not one of those who would say that Africa has gained
> nothing at all during the colonial period, I mean this is ridicu-
> lous – we have gained a lot. But unfortunately when two cul-
> tures meet, one might expect if we were angels we could
> pick out the best in the other and retain the best in our own.
> But this doesn't often happen. What happens is that some
> of the worst elements of the old are retained and some of
> the worst of the new are added, and so on. So if it were for

me to order society, I would be very unhappy at the way
things have turned out. But again, I see this is the way life is.
Every society has to grow up, every society has to learn its
own lesson.[3]

And there is, as well, a dark side to the colonial experience which
brings itself to bear as this passage reveals:

> Without subscribing to the view that Africa gained nothing at
> all in her long encounter with Europe, one could still say, in all
> fairness, that she suffered many terrible and lasting misfor-
> tunes. In terms of human dignity and human relations the
> encounter was almost a complete disaster for the black races.
> It has warped the mental attitudes of both black and white.[4]

The colonial experience, then, for Achebe created ambiguities. The
political and economic possibilities afforded by the contact with the
West are many and Achebe is optimistic about them. In human
terms the results were less than satisfactory and much of Achebe's
prose is concerned to show that African dignity, demeaned through
contact with Europe, must be reasserted. Colonialism, however,
has provided the means. Not only did colonialism unite 'many
peoples that had hitherto gone their separate ways,' it 'gave them
a language with which they could talk together'. If it failed to give
them a song, it at least gave them a tongue, for singing.[5] Achebe
distinguishes two kinds of language available to the African writers:
'ethnic language' used by and available only to 'one ethnic group
within the nation' and 'national language' which is that 'which
takes the whole nation for its province and has a realized or poten-
tial audience throughout its territory'. Achebe is concerned only
with national language (which is of course the legacy of the colonial power) and notes that national languages have been used
variously to reflect the experience of colonialism.

> In giving expression to the plight of their people, black writers
> have shown again and again how strongly this traumatic
> experience can possess the sensibility. They have found them-
> selves drawn irresistibly to writing about the fate of black
> people in a world progressively recreated by white men in
> their own image, to their glory and for their profit, in which
> the Negro became the poor motherless child of the spirituals

and of so many Nigerian folk tales. The writers' treatment of the subject has varied according to the peculiar circumstance of each particular person – his strength and his mood, to say nothing of the mood of his times. We have seen pathetic pleading, tactical acceptance, strident protest, bitter irony, assertion of non-white 'values', sometimes tentative, sometimes aggressive.[6]

But however the writer uses it, he cannot nor is it his right to dispense with the 'national language'. Just as the legacy of colonialism at the political and economic levels is something which African nations can adapt and modify for their own special needs, so the language will be used. Achebe observes:

> There are not many countries in Africa today where you could abolish the language of the erstwhile colonial powers and still retain the facility for mutual communication. Therefore those African writers who have chosen to write in English or French are not unpatriotic smart alecs with an eye on the main chance– outside their own countries. They are by-products of the same processes that made the new nation states of Africa.[7]

The important thing is not that colonialism has endowed various African writers with a world language: the important thing is how the writer uses the language. Achebe has commented on this in a variety of places and his views are perhaps best summed up in this quotation:

> . . . my answer to the question, Can an African ever learn English well enough to be able to use it effectively in creative writing? is certainly yes. If on the other hand you ask: Can he ever learn to use it like a native speaker? I should say: I hope not. It is neither necessary nor desirable for him to be able to do so. The price a world language must be prepared to pay is submission to many different kinds of use. The African writer should aim to use English in a way that brings out his message best without altering the language to the extent that its value as a medium of international exchange will be lost. He should aim at fashioning out an English which is at once universal and able to carry his peculiar experience. I have in mind here the writer who has something new, something

different to say. The nondescript writer has little to tell us anyway, so he might as well tell it in conventional language and get it over with. If I may use an extravagant simile, he is like a man offering a small, nondescript, routine sacrifice for which a chick or less will do. A serious writer must look for an animal whose blood can match the power of his offering.[8]

These comments imply that African writers are faced with difficulties not usually encountered by novelists writing in a world language, in this case English. They are in an important sense outside the literary traditions of England, America and the literary traditions of other societies and nations, which faced similar difficulties at earlier times – the Caribbean, India and certain parts of South-East Asia – whose histories in many respects are similar to that of Africa but whose traditions of imaginative writing in English have been established for several generations. Achebe looks unflinchingly at the unique position in which the African writer finds himself.

For an African, writing in English is not without its serious set-backs. He often finds himself describing situations or modes of thought which have no direct equivalent in the English way of life. Caught in that situation he can do one of two things. He can try and contain what he wants to say within the limit of conventional English or he can try to push back those limits to accommodate his ideas. The first method produces competent, uninspired and rather flat work. The second method can produce something new and valuable to the English language as well as to the material he is trying to put over. *But* it can also get out of hand. It can lead to bad English being accepted and defended as African or Nigerian. I submit that those who can do the work of extending the frontiers of English so as to accommodate African thought-patterns must do it through their mastery of English and not out of innocence.[9]

This implies more than simply using *good* English although this is an important consideration. It is important to avoid the use of *bad* English so far as Achebe is concerned because this may be 'accepted and defined as African'. And this, in turn, is important because African writing is in large part, the assertion (or reassertion) of the cultural worth of societies directed in their own language to an

overseas audience which heretofore had neither appreciated nor
acknowledged this worth. The past of various African societies
'with all its imperfections was not one long night of savagery from
which the first Europeans acting on God's behalf delivered them'.[10]
The role of the writer in a new nation, then, is partly educative,
and this, writes Achebe:

> presents the African writer with a great challenge. It is incon-
> ceivable to me that a serious writer could stand aside from this
> debate or be indifferent to this argument which calls his full
> humanity in question. For me, at any rate there is a clear duty
> to make a statement. This is my answer to those who say that a
> writer should be writing about contemporary issues – about
> politics in 1964, about city life, about the last *coup d'état*. Of
> course, these are all legitimate themes for the writer but as far
> as I am concerned the fundamental theme must first be dis-
> posed of. This theme – put quite simply – is that African people
> did not hear of culture for the first time from Europeans; that
> their societies were not mindless but frequently had a philo-
> sophy of great depth and value and beauty, that they had poetry
> and, above all, they had dignity. It is this dignity that many
> African people all but lost during the colonial period, and it is
> this that they must now regain. The worst thing that can hap-
> pen to any people is the loss of their dignity and self-respect.
> The writer's duty is to help them regain it by showing them in
> human terms what happened to them, what they lost. There is
> a saying in Ibo that a man who can't tell where the rain began
> to beat him cannot know where he dried his body. The writer
> can tell the people where the rain began to beat them.[11]

Achebe's assertions of the educative role of the writer are perhaps
best summed up in the following quotation:

> The writer cannot be excused from the task of re-education
> and re-generation that must be done. In fact he should march
> right in front. For he is after all – as Ezekiel Mphahlele says in
> his *African Image* – the sensitive point in his community. . . .
> Perhaps what I write is applied art as distinct from pure. But
> who cares? Art is important but so is education of the kind I
> have in mind.[12]

Achebe's first and third novels reflect his interest in the recent history of his people and in their traditions, cultural, religious and political. They are expressions in terms of imaginative art of the tensions, stresses and conflicts, presented in personal, social and spiritual terms, of late nineteenth- and early twentieth-century Ibo society. His own experiences account for his interest and the imaginative evocations he makes; they account as well for his formulation of the role the writer can take in the present. Achebe was born in Ogidi near Awka and not far from Onitsha on the Niger, in 1930. His father was a mission teacher, among the first of many Ibos to undertake this career. His grandfather had reached maturity by the time the first missionaries reached eastern Nigeria. Achebe's recreation of his grandfather's generation is in part reconstruction. Many changes, wrought by colonialism, had taken place in Nigeria by the time he was a schoolboy. This accounts for our saying that Achebe is a de-colonized writer, something with which he would doubtless agree. For one thing, 'although pre-colonial society had not completely disappeared' it was necessary for him to ask questions in order to 'fill in the gaps' in what was retained of traditional practises. For another thing, as a Christian he was excluded from certain activities practised by non-Christians.

> On looking back, if I had an advantage, it was that my father was a retired missionary when I was growing up; wc were Christians and in our village you had two sides – the 'people of the Church', as we were called, and the 'people of the world', the others. Although we were in the same village there was a certain distance which I think made it possible for me not to take things for granted. I say this because some of the people who grew up with me, whose parents were heathen, as we called them, these things did not strike them. At least this is what they tell me today – they took things for granted.[13]

His education at Government Secondary School at Umuahia and later at the University College of Ibadan, where he was among the first graduates, brought him into further and more intense contact with European culture and especially with European literary traditions and analytical critical attitudes. At the same time his interest in the recent history of Nigeria continued to grow and the result is imaginative writing of concreteness gained through strict precision and control which views objectively the forces which irresistibly and inevitably destroyed traditional Ibo society, writing which avoids the temptation to present this past as idealized, This latter is the most serious of the temptations to which the writer who undertakes the task of asserting the worth and value of his traditional society is subject:

> The question is how does a writer re-create this past? Quite clearly there is a strong temptation to idealize it – to extol its good points and pretend that the bad never existed.
> This is where the writer's integrity comes in. Will he be strong enough to overcome the temptation to select only those facts which flatter him? If he succumbs he will have branded himself as an untrustworthy witness. But it is not only his personal integrity as an artist which is involved. The credibility of the world he is attempting to recreate will be called to question and he will defeat his own purpose if he is suspected of glossing over inconvenient facts. We cannot pretend that our past was one long, technicolour idyll. We have to admit that like other people's pasts ours had its good as well as its bad sides.[14]

As an interpreter of the cultural worth of his own society and as critic of the quality of that life, Achebe is no different than other writers in other places and times. And like them his claim to being a novelist in the fullest sense of the word does not rest on his success within this limited area of the novelist's function. In the long run it is the art that matters. Many commentators have reacted to his novels primarily as social documents and praised their 'anthropological' and 'sociological' content. There is nothing wrong with having 'anthropological' or 'sociological' biases and making judgements based upon them. But these are not literary judgements and they have nothing to do with the achievement of novels as works of literature. The sociology and anthropology in Achebe's work provides its background, and background, carefully and convincingly evoked, is important to the success of his novels. But it is never allowed to dominate the human life the novels reveal. Like any other, African fiction will achieve universality through both a sensitive rendering and interpretation of its own culture and through transcending the purely local conditions which occasion it. Achebe recognizes this when he says: 'The writer's duty is not to beat this morning's headlines in topicality; it is to explore the depth of the human condition.'[15]

To interpret Achebe's work as mere explication of the Nigerian scene, either that of his grandfather's or his own generation, is to mistake his intention and his achievement. In kind with most writers of his generation, he has shown in his published novels and short stories a pre-occupation with certain basic themes, of which the legacy of colonial rule is the central core. It is true that the novels reveal the destructive consequences of the rule of the colonial period. But these are not displayed for their own sake. They are there because they arise out of and reflect to a sensitive mind a manifest indifference and caprice which mirrors life itself. This pre-occupation is found in each of the novels as Achebe explores its meaning and seeks to accommodate himself to it. The heroes of the first three novels have their origins in this. These heroes, conceived in tragic terms, are men in varying degrees conscious of the fact that life turns out to be less manageable and less perfect than they had expected, they react to life in various ways – with courage, honesty and generosity, with pessimism and cynicism – in their attempts to get through life with honour and reward.

It can be argued that for Achebe the principal virtue is to accept stoically what life serves up. But his pre-occupation is more than this: it is with the plight of the individual in a world characterized by uncertainty, pain and violence. Achebe is essentially a moralist, concerned with considerations of right and wrong as they are revealed by the individual's responses to the circumstances which surround him. This has not been generally understood partly as has been suggested because his novels bring news of strange parts of the world to many readers and considerations of background attract undue attention, and partly because his method as an artist is one of implication rather than explication. It is rarely that he intrudes himself between his reader and his work. His typical method is based on allusion and implication which leaves much unsaid and thus his writing achieves a suggestiveness which communicates far more than he might achieve in long passages of explicit description. Achebe, through this method, causes the reader to identify with the actions and reactions of the characters and make the same discoveries about the nature of things as the characters themselves.

B

To his single-minded striving for perfection are added the qualities of a judgement which perceives the essentials of a scene or
action; a perceptiveness about people and how they think, feel
and react, and an extraordinary skill in the use of dialogue. His
work displays a vision of life, remote from that of many of his
readers, even within Africa, which nevertheless comes to bear
directly on matters of fundamental importance to the majority of
his contemporaries. Above all he is a serious and dedicated artist:

> The writer in our society should be able to think of these things
> [the causes for and implications of many kinds of different ac-
> tions in the contemporary scene] and bring them out in a form
> that is dramatic and memorable. Above all he has a responsibi-
> lity to avoid shoddiness in his work. This is very important to-
> day when some publishers will issue any trash that comes out
> of Africa because Africa has become the fashion. In this situa-
> tion there is a real danger that some writers may not be patient
> enough and disciplined enough to pursue excellence in their
> work. . . . African societies of the past, with all their imperfec-
> tions, were not consumers but producers of culture. Anyone
> who reads Fagg's recent book *Nigerian Images* will be struck
> by the wealth and quality of the art our ancestors produced in
> the past. Some of this work played a decisive role in the history
> of modern art. The time has come once more for us, artists and
> writers of today, to take up the good work and by doing it we
> will enrich not only our own lives but the life of the world.[16]

Things Fall Apart

▼▼▼▼▼▼▼▼▼▼▼▼▼▼▼▼▼▼▼▼▼▼▼▼▼▼▼▼▼▼

T HINGS FALL APART, like all first-rate works of fiction, is at once concrete and general: in looking at *Things Fall
Apart* we recognize its Africanness and yet are able to see its
universal implications: it is one of those works which in realizing its
environment to the full achieves universality. It is about Iboland,
in the eastern region of present-day Nigeria, in the period between
1850–1900; that is, the period just prior to and after the arrival of
white men in this part of West Africa. The people, the novel reveals, live not in some vaguely defined part of Africa but in Umuofia and Mbanta, the two principal villages in a union called the
'nine villages'. Okonkwo, the hero of the novel, a great wrestler in
his youth, is, when we meet him, a renowned warrior (celebrated in
praise songs at religious festivals) and one of the most wealthy,
powerful and influential members of Umuofia. The language of
Okonkwo and the other villagers is expressed in the idiom of the
Ibo villagers as Achebe transmutes it into modern English. The
story of *Things Fall Apart* is concerned with the passions of living
people, with the validity of traditional religion, with property
ownership, with the relations between the rich and the poor, with
the arrangements of marriages and the celebrations of deaths. The
conflict in the novel, vested in Okonkwo, derives from the series
of crushing blows which are levelled at traditional values by an alien
and more powerful culture causing, in the end, the traditional
society to fall apart. Thus the significance of the title of the book
taken from Yeats's *The Second Coming*:

> Turning and turning in the widening gyre
> The falcon cannot hear the falconer;
> Things fall apart; the centre cannot hold;
> Mere anarchy is loosed upon the world.

In his evocation of his grandfather's generation Achebe achieves concreteness and convincingness through strict precision and control. We experience the forces of nature at work in the novel – the searing heat of the dry season, the bitter cold of the harmattan, the relentless downpour of the rainy season – and we appreciate their elemental quality because the life of the people in all its variety is governed by the seasons.

It is necessary to stress this point about the novel since much has been made about this aspect of Achebe's writing: the background of *Things Fall Apart*, however concrete and detailed, however thorough in its delineation of the total cultural pattern of nineteenth-century Ibo life, has not become the subject of the book. The strength of the novel partly lies in its naturalistic description and its detailed presentation and analysis of the day by day and hour by hour issues of social living. But while he works at the level of ideas, Achebe also works at the level of symbols – that is, the level of concepts which have significance and validity on a level different from that of logical thought.

Things Fall Apart is a vision of what life was like in Iboland between 1850 and 1900. Achebe makes a serious attempt to capture realistically the strains and tensions of the experiences of Ibo people under the impact of colonialism. What ultimately gives this novel its strength is Achebe's feelings for the plight and problems of these peoples. It is not wholly true, however, to say that the novel is written consistently from their point of view. Achebe is a twentieth-century Ibo man, a de-colonized writer, and recognizes the wide gulf which exists between his present-day society and that of Ibo villagers sixty years ago, sixty years which have seen remarkable changes in the texture and structure of Ibo society.

Achebe is able to view objectively the forces which irresistibly and inevitably destroyed traditional Ibo social ties and with them the quality of Ibo life. In showing Ibo society before and after the coming of the white man he avoids the temptation to present the past as idealized and the present as ugly and unsatisfactory. The atmosphere of the novel is realistic and not romantic, although there are romantic elements in it. Put another way, Achebe manages to express a romantic vision of Ibo life in realistic form, to encompass aspects of that life which evoke it in all its complexity and convincingness. Achebe's success proceeds not from his interest in the history of his people and their folklore and legend in an academic sense, even though he puts these to good use in the novel, nor from the fact that he tells a compelling story, although this is true. His success proceeds from his ability to create a sense of real life and real issues in the book and to see his subject from a point of view which is neither idealistic nor dishonest. Of the temptation to present the past in an idealized form, especially to the African writer, Achebe has written:

> . . . the past needs to be recreated not only for the enlighten-ment of our detractors but even more for our own educa-tion. Because . . . the past with all its imperfections, never lacked dignity. . . . This is where the writer's integrity comes in. Will he be strong enough to overcome the tempt-ation to select only those facts which flatter him? If he succumbs he will have branded himself as an untrustworthy witness. But it is not only his personal integrity as an artist which is involved. The credibility of the world he is attempting to recreate will be called to question and he will defeat his own purpose if he is suspected of glossing over inconvenient facts.[17]

Things Fall Apart is a small book which for all its apparent casualness and sobriety of style and the complexity of the human relationships it presents, is a very well-constructed book, in which technical problems of presentation have been most carefully worked out. Further, Achebe's method of working affects complete verisi-militude in its presentation: he never imposes himself between us and the scene he presents. Achebe is the most objective of writers in this sense.

Things Fall Apart has three sections or parts to it: the first and most important is set in Umuofia before the coming of the white man – before his existence is even known. The second part drama-tizes Okonkwo's banishment to Mbanta, the village of his mother's people, for sins committed against the Earth Goddess, and des-cribes, mostly through reports, the coming of the white man to the nine villages and the establishment of an alien church, government and trading system and the gradual encroachment of these on the traditional patterns of tribal life. The third section and the

shortest brings the novel swiftly to a close, dramatizing the death
of the old ways and the death of Okonkwo.

Achebe's prose has been described as 'leisurely' and 'stately'
and a casual reading of the book, especially the first part, supports
such judgement. Because Achebe refuses to take sides in the issues
he describes and dramatizes, his presentation is disinterested and
this quality is reflected in the writing. Yet, restrained as the pace
may be, it moves the story forward with a sense of inevitability,
the momentum gradually increasing until the first climax is
reached, Okonkwo's third sin against the Earth Goddess and his
subsequent banishment. The casual approach and style quite belie
the intensity of the life the novel evokes and from the outset
Achebe's absolute certainty of approach is established. Umuofia is
an organic unity. It is a place where people live, a community, a
centre of co-operating and conflicting men and women, which
achieves an identity of its own. Moreover, it is unified by an Ibo
consciousness and achieves a rich ambiguity which refers ultimately not only to Umuofia and the nine villages but to all of Iboland at this particular point in time.

At the centre of the community is Okonkwo, a character of intense individuality, yet one in whom the values most admired by
Ibo peoples are consolidated. He is both an individual and a type.
The first paragraphs of the book indicate the deftness and certainty
with which Achebe establishes not only the character but the ethical
and moral basis of his life and, by extension, the ethical and moral
basis of the life of the clan.

> Okonkwo was well known throughout the nine villages and
> even beyond. His fame rested on solid personal achievements.
> As a young man of eighteen he had brought honour to his
> village by throwing Amalinze the Cat. Amalinze was the
> greatest wrestler who for seven years was unbeaten, from
> Umuofia to Mbaino. . . . In the end Okonkwo threw the Cat.
>
> That was many years ago, twenty or more, and during this
> time Okonkwo's fame had grown like a bush fire in the harmat-
> tan. . . . When he walked, his heels barely touched the ground
> and he seemed to walk on springs, as if he was going to pounce
> on somebody. And he did pounce on people quite often. He had
> a slight stammer and whenever he could not get his words out

quickly enough, he would use his fists. He had no patience
with unsuccessful men. He had no patience with his father.*

In extrapolating sentences out of context one often does an
author a disservice. Full exegesis of the first chapter would reveal
an even greater complexity of meaning and richness of texture in
the prose. The passages cited above reveal precisely at the outset
of the novel the premium which is placed on wealth, courage and
valour among the Ibo people. Okonkwo was 'clearly cut out for
great things' but he had earned his reputation, as a wrestler (he
brought fame to himself and his village); as a warrior (he had taken
the approved symbols of his prowess, the heads of five victims by the
time he was twenty-one years old); as a man who had achieved
personal wealth symbolized by his two barns full of yams, his
three wives and, of great importance, the two titles he had taken,
titles which can only be acquired when wealth has been achieved
and quality proven.

Okonkwo was 'one of the greatest men of his time', the embodiment of Ibo values, the man who better than most symbolized his
race. His stature is presented as heroic. His story, as was men-
tioned above, is presented in terms which resemble those of Aristotelian tragedy – the working out in the life of a hero of industry,
courage and eminence, of an insistent fatality (in this book symbolized by the *chi*, or personal god) which transcends his ability
to fully understand or resist a fore-ordained sequence of events.
Achebe suggests as well the flaw, or flaws in his nature – his inordinate ambition and his refusal to tolerate anything less than excellence, taken in conjunction with an impulsive rage to which he
easily gives way and which produces irrational responses to situations. In this connection the comment that Okonkwo had 'no
patience with his father' is important, for Unoka, the father,
represents everything which Okonkwo personally despises and
his life embodies the antithesis of those values most cherished by
the Ibo people. We are told that Unoka was 'poor and his wife
and children had barely enough to eat', that he was 'lazy and

* Achebe, Chinua, *Things Fall Apart*, Heinemann Educational Books
1962, pp. 3–4. All further page references in this chapter are to this edition. For those with a cased edition of *Things Fall Apart* page numbers are
two less than those quoted here.

improvident', a 'debtor' and a 'coward who could not stand the sight of blood'. Achebe characterizes him deftly in this passage:

> [Unoka] would remember his own childhood, how he had often wandered around looking for a kite sailing leisurely against the blue sky. As soon as he found one he would sing with his whole being, welcoming it back from its long, long journey, and asking it if it had brought home any lengths of cloth. (p. 5.)

His capacity to day-dream, his laziness and improvidence – his childish hope that the kite would bring back cloth and thus absolve him from the necessity of providing for himself – are summed up in this anecdote, which is not without charm, and his character is made to stand in direct contrast to Okonkwo's and to enhance his central position in the book. This is made explicit in the second chapter of the book:

> [Okonkwo's] whole life was dominated by fear, the fear of failure and weakness. It was deeper and more intimate than the fear of evil and capricious gods and of magic, the fear of the forest and of the forces of nature, malevolent, red in tooth and claw. Okonkwo's fear was greater than these. It was not external but lay deep within himself. It was the fear of himself, lest he should be found to resemble his father. Even as a little boy he had resented his father's failure and weakness, and even now he still remembered how he had suffered when a playmate told him that his father was *agbala*. That was how Okonkwo first came to know that *agbala* was not only another name for a woman, it could also mean a man who had taken no title. And so Okonkwo was ruled by one passion – to hate everything that his father Unoka had loved. One of those things was gentleness and another was idleness. (pp. 12–13.)

The passages cited above suggest Achebe's sensitive yet unobtrusive use of English to reflect the African environment and to integrate character and incident through the use of imagery drawn from traditional sources, a technique so consistent in its application that it can be demonstrated in passages taken from any part of the novel. On the first page of the novel we are told that 'Okonkwo's fame had grown like a bush-fire in the harmattan'. A few pages farther along the following metaphor is offered: 'Among the Ibo the art of conversation is regarded very highly, and proverbs are the palm-oil with which words are eaten.' (p. 6.) Both images it is important to note are drawn from nature – palm-oil and harmattan – indicating the connection between human life and the soil. The reference to proverbs in the second selection is important since Achebe incorporates much proverbial material couched in traditional verbal formulae, again naturally and with a sense of exact appropriateness. In the third chapter of the novel where Achebe describes Okonkwo's visit to a wealthy man of the village to seek his help, the following passage occurs, displaying the dramatic function Achebe makes of proverbial materials:

'I have come to you for help,' he said. 'Perhaps you can already guess what it is. I have cleared a farm but have no yams to sow. I know what it is to ask a man to trust another with his yams, especially these days when young men are afraid of hard work. I am not afraid of hard work. The lizard that jumped from the high iroko tree to the ground said he would praise himself if no one else did. I began to fend for myself at an age when most people still suck at their mothers' breasts. If you give me some yam seeds I shall not fail you.'

Nwakibie cleared his throat. 'It pleases me to see a young man like you these days when our youth have gone so soft. Many young men come to me to ask for yams but I have refused because I knew they would just dump them in the earth and leave them to be choked by weeds. When I say no to them they think I am hard-hearted. But it is not so. Eneke the bird says that since men have learned to shoot without missing, he has learnt to fly without perching. I have learned to be stingy with my yams. But I can trust you. I know it as I look at you. As our fathers said, you can tell a ripe corn by its look. I shall give you twice four hundred yams. Go and prepare your farm.' (p. 20.)

The passage concludes with the observation 'Yam, the king of crops, was a man's crop.'

The images again are chosen from nature and suggest the continuum of the natural world of which man is part and at the centre. There are several references in this passage which require further comment because they lead into a deeper consideration of the way in which Achebe uses environment not only to symbolize character and theme, but also to define the moral and ethical principles on which Ibo society is based and which is his ultimate concern in the book.

The yam is king: a man's wealth, status and reputation depend upon his possession of yams. Yams are food, true, and 'he who could feed his family on yams from one harvest to another was a very great man indeed'. But, as well, 'yams stood for manliness'. With yams, which are wealth, a man could take titles in the clan; that is, he could achieve power and influence the conduct of the affairs of the clan. Conversely a man without yams was not able to take titles: he is described as *agbala* a word which as we have seen denotes 'a woman' and a man without titles. The two concepts are linked: to possess a female disposition is undesirable if not wholly unacceptable. Yet in the opposition between the man who possesses yams and the one who does not a paradox is apparent. While a continuing emphasis on male activities – acquisition of wealth and wives, the production of children, courage and resourcefulness in sport and war – informs the surface interest of the novel, all activity in *Things Fall Apart* is judged by what is or is not acceptable to 'Ani, the Earth Goddess and source of all fertility,' . . . 'ultimate judge of morality and conduct' (p. 33) in the clan. In other words a powerful 'female principle' pervades the whole society of Umuofia and sits in judgement of events in the community. This is conveyed in one of the most impressive scenes in the book, the scene in which Chielo, priestess and oracle to Ani, borrows Ezinma, Okonkwo's daughter by his second wife Ekwefi. Ekwefi has been afflicted by a series of still-births and dreads the loss of Ezinma, the only child to survive. She approaches despair as she follows the priestess through the nine villages where Ani's power over life and death is successively proclaimed. We are made to feel Ekwefi's terror of a world 'peopled with vague, fantastic figures that dissolved under her gaze and then formed again in new shapes'. And the omnipotence of the Goddess is ultimately suggested by the change her influence works on the woman who is Her priestess.

. . . at that very moment Chielo's voice rose again in her possessed chanting, and Ekwefi recoiled, because there was no humanity there. It was not the same Chielo who sat with her in the market place and sometimes bought bean-cakes for Ezinma, whom she called her daughter. It was a different woman – the priestess of Agbala, the Oracle of the Hills and Caves. (p. 97.)

The woman's world is normally benign: but this central scene in the first part of the novel dramatizes the essential power who governs and controls the society. Powerful as he is, the embodiment of the male principle, Okonkwo is subservient to the female principle and he follows the course of Chielo with his beloved daughter Ezinma with a terror equal to that of his wife, utterly powerless to alter the course of events.

Okonkwo's downfall and eventual banishment from the tribe at the end of the first part of the novel proceeds from offences committed 'against the earth'. The first occurs during a week of peace when he beats his wife for her fecklessness. Characteristically impulsive, Okonkwo was not one to let fear of a goddess stand in his way (p. 27). For this offence Ani demands retribution in the form of money which Okonkwo pays. The second offence relates to the killing of Ikemefuna, a boy-hostage taken from a neighbouring clan and placed in Okonkwo's household. Ikemefuna becomes as a son to Okonkwo. Nwoye, Okonkwo's eldest son and a source of grave concern to Okonkwo because he shows all the signs of possessing the 'female' disposition of his grandfather, thrives under the influence of Ikemefuna – Nwoye, we are told, 'grows like a yam tendril in the rainy season'. The deity eventually decrees that Ikemefuna must be killed. Okonkwo is warned that he must take no hand in the killing. Yet for fear of appearing weak and cowardly Okonkwo cuts down Ikemefuna with his matchet.

One of the men behind him cleared his throat. Ikemefuna looked back, and the man growled at him to go on and not stand looking back. The way he said it sent cold fear down Ikemefuna's back. His hands trembled vaguely on the black pot he carried. Why had Okonkwo withdrawn to the rear? Ikemefuna felt his legs melting under him. And he was afraid to look back.

As the man who had cleared his throat drew up and raised his matchet, Okonkwo looked away. He heard the blow. The

pot fell and broke in the sand. He heard Ikemefuna cry, 'My
father, they have killed me!' as he ran towards him. Dazed
with fear, Okonkwo drew his matchet and cut him down. He
was afraid of being thought weak. (pp. 54–5.)

The scene is rendered by Achebe with a terseness which makes
the horror of it all the more compelling. Yet the special horror is
not that Okonkwo has killed this boy whom he has grown to love –
the authority and decision of the Oracle are not questioned – but,
as Okonkwo's friend Obierika says with a voice prophetic of the
doom which will overtake Okonkwo, his is the 'kind of action for
which the goddess wipes out whole families.' (p. 61.)

The crime for which he is eventually exiled is that of accidentally
killing the son of a kinsman whose funeral observances Okonkwo
attends. Okonkwo and his gun have been the subject of an earlier
episode which has provided Achebe with the opportunity for an
interesting exercise in irony. Okonkwo has beaten his wife for
destroying a banana tree:

> His anger thus satisfied, Okonkwo decided to go out hunting.
> He had an old rusty gun made by a clever blacksmith who had
> come to live in Umuofia long ago. But although Okonkwo was
> a great man whose prowess was universally acknowledged, he
> was not a hunter. In fact he had not killed a rat with his gun.
> And so when he called Ikemefuna to fetch his gun, the wife
> who had just been beaten murmured something about guns
> that never shot. Unfortunately for her, Okonkwo heard it and
> ran madly into his room for the loaded gun, ran out again and
> aimed at her as she clambered over the dwarf wall of the barn.
> He pressed the trigger and there was a loud report accom-
> panied by the wail of his wives and children. He threw down
> the gun and jumped into the barn, and there lay the woman,
> very much shaken and frightened but quite unhurt. He heaved
> a heavy sigh and went away with the gun. (pp. 35–6.)

Had Okonkwo been a hunter and skilled shot his wife, because of
his inordinate rage, would most certainly have been killed. The
irony is that when killing is farthest from Okonkwo's mind his
gun explodes killing a kinsman, a sin he must expiate through
exile.

The only course open to Okonkwo was to flee from the clan. It was a crime against the earth goddess to kill a clansman, and a man who committed it must flee from the land. The crime was of two kinds, male and female. Okonkwo had committed the female, because it was inadvertent. He could return to the clan after seven years. . . .

That night he collected his most valuable belongings into head-loads. . . . And before the cock crowed Okonkwo and his family were fleeing to his motherland. . . .

As soon as the day broke, a large crowd of men from Ezeudu's quarter stormed Okonkwo's compound, dressed in garbs of war. They set fire to his houses, demolished his red walls, killed his animals and destroyed his barn. It was the justice of the earth goddess, and they were merely her messengers. They had no hatred in their hearts against Okonkwo. His greatest friend, Obierika, was among them. They were merely cleansing the land which Okonkwo had polluted with the blood of a clansman.

Obierika was a man who thought about things. When the will of the goddess had been done, he sat down in his *obi* and mourned his friend's calamity. Why should a man suffer so grievously for an offence he had committed inadvertently? But although he thought for a long time he found no answer. He was merely led into greater complexities. He remembered his wife's twin children whom he had thrown away. What crime had they committed? The Earth had decreed that they were an offence on the land and must be destroyed. And if the clan did not exact punishment for an offence against the great goddess, her wrath was loosed on all the land and not just on the offender. As the elders said, if one finger brought oil it soiled the others. (pp. 113–14.)

At this moment the female principle is invoked in the novel. It is not scrutinized nor explained beyond the superficial level indicated in Obierika's musing: it is the accepted moral and ethical basis of the clan and is consistently observed. The close dramatization of the female principle virtually disappears from the second part of the book, to be invoked again in the final section and made to account for the novel's tragic resolution.

The first part of the novel is on the surface a loosely ordered series of incidents – the throwing of the Cat, the killing of Ikemefuna, the shot fired at Ekwefi and the haunting pilgrimage of Chielo. What it establishes in fact, through a patina of images, similes and metaphors, proverbs and legend, is the symbolic and moral continuity of the life of the clan against which the action of the second and third parts of the novel is played out.

In the second and third parts of the novel the critical social conflict takes place. These sections present the social and psychological effects and the tragic consequences which result from the clash between traditional Ibo society and British Christian Imperialism. In the second section, as well, the relationship between Okonkwo and his refractory son Nwoye is delineated in such a way as to transmute the broader cultural conflict to the personal level.

Okonkwo is well-received by his mother's people in the village of Mbanta to which he goes in his banishment. The female principle within the tribal ethic is apparent. Okonkwo's offence has been against the Earth Goddess and forced his exile. Yet it is to the mother's village he proceeds. Uchendu, his mother's youngest brother and now an old man, explains the rationale:

> It's true that a child belongs to its father. But when a father beats his child, it seeks sympathy in its mother's hut. A man belongs to his fatherland when things are good and life is sweet. But when there is sorrow and bitterness he finds refuge in his motherland. Your mother is there to protect you. She is buried there. And that is why we say that mother is supreme. (p. 122.)

Though disappointed and disillusioned by the blows fate has dealt him Okonkwo begins with characteristic single-mindedness to build a new life for himself along the same principles as he applied in his youth, and to plan against his return to Umuofia seven years hence.

> Okonkwo and his family worked very hard to plant a new farm. But it was like beginning life anew without the vigour and enthusiasm of youth, like learning to become left-handed in old age. Work no longer had for him the pleasure it used to have, and when there was no work to do he sat in a silent half-sleep.

His life had been ruled by a great passion – to become one of the lords of the clan. That had been his life-spring. And he had all but achieved it. Then everything had been broken. He had been cast out of his clan, like a fish on to a dry, sandy beach, panting. Clearly his personal god or *chi* was not made for great things. A man could not rise above the destiny of his *chi*. The saying of the elders was not true – that if a man said yea his *chi* also affirmed. Here was a man whose *chi* said nay despite his own affirmation. (pp. 118–19.)

The reference to the *chi* is important. Okonkwo's achievement has been heroic – he almost reached the summit of his ambition to become one of the lords of the clan. But his destiny is otherwise: this he now suspects. When Obierika had prophesied doom for Okonkwo at the time of the killing of Ikemefuna, the implications were lost to Okonkwo. Now he himself begins to suspect that he is in the grip of an overriding destiny which he cannot control. Placed here at the time of his despair, and despite his resolve to return to Umuofia and achieve his fullest desires, the fact that his *chi* says 'nay' indicates his position as tragic hero and foreshadows his tragic end.

Achebe tells the story of the coming of the white men – at first the missionaries and then, close behind, the civil administrators, soldiers and traders – with characteristic economy and restraint which belie the complexity of the issues involved, a complexity which is directly reflected in the structure of the novel. Obierika makes two visits to Okonkwo during the latter's exile. During the first visit he reveals, almost casually, that Abame, one of the villages in the union of the nine villages, 'is no more'. Recording the tale of refugees who had come to Umuofia from Abame Obierika says:

'During the last planting season a white man had appeared in their clan.'
'An albino,' suggested Okonkwo.
'He was not an albino. He was quite different.' He sipped his wine. 'And he was riding an iron horse. The first people who saw him ran away, but he stood beckoning to them. In the end the fearless ones went near and even touched him. The elders consulted their Oracle and it told them that the strange man would break their clan and spread destruction among

them.' Obierika again drank a little of his wine. 'And so they killed the white man and tied his iron horse to their sacred tree because it looked as if it would run away to call the man's friends. I forgot to tell you another thing which the Oracle said. It said that other white men were on their way. They were locusts, it said, and that first man was their harbinger sent to explore the terrain. . . . Anyway . . . they killed him and tied up his iron horse. This was before the planting season began. For a long time nothing happened. The rains had come and the yams had been sown. The iron horse was still tied to the sacred silk-cotton tree. And then one morning three white men led by a band of ordinary men like us came to the clan. They saw the iron horse and went away again. . . . For many market weeks nothing else happened. They have a big market in Abame on every other Afo day and, as you know, the whole clan gathers there. That was the day it happened. The three white men and a very large band of other men surrounded the market. They must have used a powerful medicine to make themselves invisible until the market was full. And they began to shoot. Everybody was killed, except the old and the sick who were at home and a handful of men and women whose *chi* were wide awake and brought them out of the market.' (pp. 125–6.)

Here again the consistency of Achebe's approach to his art is revealed. The image of the 'iron horse' (a bicycle) is central for through its use Achebe is able to suggest the differences in ideas and understanding which existed between the two systems by presenting them in the idiom of the Ibo people. In this way he is able to prepare the way for showing the lack of understanding which will characterize his elaboration of the wider ideological beliefs between the two systems. Grave concern over the event is expressed by Uchendu who says 'Never kill a man who says nothing. Those men of Abame were fools. What did they know about the man?' (p. 126.) Okonkwo and Obierika are less alarmed and the episode closes on an almost whimsical note. Obierika says he has sold some of Okonkwo's yams and brought him the money. 'Who knows what may happen tomorrow,' he says. 'Perhaps green men will come to our clan and shoot us.' (p. 128.)

The situation has altered entirely when Obierika makes his next visit to Okonkwo. We are told, quite matter-of-factly:

> The missionaries had come to Umuofia. They had built their church there, won a handful of converts and were already sending evangelists to the surrounding towns and villages. (p. 130.)

At first their appeal is to the wrong kind of people and they are not feared:

> None of his converts was a man whose word was heeded in the assembly of the people. . . . They were mostly the kind of people that were called *efulefu*, worthless, empty men. The imagery of an *efulefu* in the language of the clan was a man who sold his matchet and wore the sheath to battle. (p. 130.)

This chapter, sixteen, and the two which follow describe the vicissitudes of the missionaries and how they overcame them. At first they are treated casually by the Ibo people. Eventually their evangelists arrive at Mbanta and Okonkwo pauses to listen to them in the market square 'in the hope that it might come to chasing the men out of the village or whipping them'. 'But in the end Okonkwo was fully convinced that the man was mad. He shrugged his shoulders and went away to tap his afternoon palm-wine.' (pp. 133-4.)

Such is not the case with Nwoye, Okonkwo's son. Nwoye, under the influence and companionship of Ikemefuna had grown towards manhood, when the latter was killed 'felt something give way inside him like the snapping of a tightened bow'. Now he is captivated by the new religion.

> It was not the mad logic of the Trinity that captivated him. He did not understand it. It was the poetry of the new religion, something felt in the marrow. The hymn about brothers who sat in darkness and in fear seemed to answer a vague and persistent question that haunted his young soul – the question of the twins crying in the bush and the question of Ikemefuna who was killed. He felt a relief within as the hymn poured into his parched soul. The words of the hymn were like the drops of frozen rain melting on the dry palate of the panting earth. (p. 134.)

Through Nwoye's conversion, or disaffection, Achebe focuses the wider social conflict between the two different ways of life at the personal level.

> Why, [Okonkwo] cried in his heart, should he . . . of all people, be cursed with such a son? He saw clearly in it the finger of his personal god or *chi*. For how else could he explain his great misfortune and exile and now his despicable son's behaviour? Now that he had time to think of it, his son's crime stood out in its stark enormity. To abandon the gods of one's fathers and go about with a lot of effeminate men clucking like old hens was the very depth of abomination. Suppose when he died all his male children decided to follow Nwoye's steps and abandon their ancestors? Okonkwo felt a cold shudder run through him at the terrible prospect, like the prospect of annihilation. (p. 139.)

He takes a measure of comfort when he realizes that in his youth he was called 'Roaring Flame'. And with the recognition that 'living fire begets cold, impotent ash' he is able to dismiss Nwoye from his thoughts thenceforward. But the way has been prepared for the inevitable clash between Okonkwo, symbolizing the traditional way of life, and the new order, symbolized by the Christian Church. Nwoye's conversion is told in specific and emotional terms which describe a father's reactions to the unacceptable actions of his son. But Nwoye's conversion is also symptomatic of the way in which Christianity strikes against the things Okonkwo represents. As one critic comments:

> Nwoye's defection to Christianity has a double significance – it is at the same time a revolt against his father as well as a rejection of the society that he embodied. . . . Nwoye . . . stands as a symbolic rejection of the father, the living denial of all that Okonkwo accepts and stands for.[18]

The third part of the novel begins by describing Okonkwo's return to Umuofia after his seven years of exile:

> He knew that he had lost his place among the nine masked spirits who administered justice in the clan. He had lost the chance to lead his war-like clan against the new religion,

which, he was told, had gained ground. He had lost the years in which he might have taken the highest titles in the clan. But some of these losses were not irreparable. He was determined that his return should be marked by his people. He would return with a flourish, and regain the seven wasted years. (p. 155.)

His return is less auspicious than he hoped it would be, but he bears it well. Again Achebe emphasizes the heroic stature of Okonkwo: he has withstood reversals of fortune and personal calamities which would have crushed a less resilient spirit. Significantly Achebe writes 'It seemed to him as if his *chi* might be making amends for past disasters.'

Umuofia has changed more than Okonkwo had been prepared for. Obierika sums up the change in the following passage, when Okonkwo asks:

'Does the white man understand our customs about land?'
'How can he when he does not even speak our tongue? But he says our customs are bad; and our own brothers who have taken up his religion also say that our customs are bad. How do you think we can fight when our own brothers have turned against us? The white man is very clever. He came quietly and peaceably with his religion. We were amused at his foolishness and allowed him to stay.' (p. 160.)

This passage closes with an image which is reminiscent of the breaking of kola. References are made to kola throughout the novel. Kola nut is offered to members who attend formal and informal gatherings and symbolizes for the Ibo people the continuity of tribal life. We find, throughout the book, such comments as 'he who brings kola brings life' and 'the kola was given to him and he prayed to the ancestors. . . . He then broke the kola and threw one of the lobes on the ground for the ancestors.' The breaking and sharing of kola symbolizes unity and it is a mark of the subtlety of Achebe's art that when Obierika tells Okonkwo of the disruptive influence of the missionaries on the clan he does so in a language which suggests the act of breaking kola:

Now he has won our brothers, and our clan can no longer act like one. He has put a knife on the things that held us together and we have fallen apart. (p. 160.)

Not only has the white man brought a 'lunatic religion' but 'he had also built a trading store and for the first time palm-oil and kernel became things of great price, and much money flowed into Umuofia'. (p. 161.) It is the religious principles embodied in Christianity which Okonkwo sees as the force that changes the nature of village life. His fear at the time of Nwoye's defection has now become a reality. He remains firm to the old ways, joins an attack which is made against the Christian Church and for this, with several others, is arrested by the District Commissioner and placed in irons in the jail. His sense of humiliation precipitates his final actions which culminate in his death.

But it is not the alien religion alone which accounts for the destruction of the old ways and causes them to fall apart. Rather it is a combination of factors, one of which is the new religion, the other of which is trade. The new faith possesses an appeal sufficiently strong to challenge and undermine the old religion. At the same time, through the incentives of the new value placed on palm-oil and palm kernels, the acquisitive nature of the society gains precedence. The traditional balance is upset. The male principle of acquisitiveness for the first time gains precedence over the female which heretofore provided the ethical and moral basis of conduct and acted as a restraint on the male principle. Achebe has written in this connection:

> Ibo society has always been materialistic. This may sound strange because Ibo life had at the same time a strong spiritual dimension – controlled by gods, ancestors, personal spirits or *chi* and magic. The success of the culture was the balance between the two, the material and the spiritual. . . . Today we have kept the materialism and thrown away the spirituality which should keep it in check.[19]

Achebe situates the novel in the moment of time when this destructive process began and his dramatization of it reveals not only the consistency of his vision of this change wrought at the symbolic level but also the consistency and coherence of his moral theme.

The final pages of the novel, pages once more of seeming simplicity of statement, bring the novel to a close. Okonkwo prepares for the last day of his life filled with deep foreboding and brooding nostalgia:

Okonkwo slept very little that night. The bitterness in his heart was now mixed with a kind of child-like excitement. Before he had gone to bed he had brought down his war dress, which he had not touched since his return from exile. He had shaken out his smoked raffia skirt and examined his tall feather head-gear and his shield. They were all satisfactory, he had thought.

As he lay on his bamboo bed he thought about the treatment he had received in the white man's court, and he swore vengeance. If Umuofia decided on war, all would be well. But if they chose to be cowards he would go out and avenge himself. He thought about wars in the past. (p. 179.)

At first it seems as if the gathered remnant of the clan share Okonkwo's feelings and that some decisive action will be taken. Okika, a 'great man and an orator' begins to speak:

We who are here this morning have remained true to our fathers, but our brothers have deserted us and joined a stranger to soil their fatherland. If we fight the stranger we shall hit our brothers and perhaps shed the blood of a clansman. But we must do it. . . . We must root out this evil. And if our brothers take the side of evil we must root them out too. . . . (p. 183.)

The meeting is interrupted by the sudden appearance of white authority in the person of the court messenger. Okonkwo, 'trembling with hate, unable to utter a word', drew his matchet.

The messenger crouched to avoid the blow. It was useless. Okonkwo's matchet descended twice and the man's head lay beside his uniformed body.

The waiting backcloth jumped into tumultuous life and the meeting was stopped. Okonkwo stood looking at the dead man. He knew that Umuofia would not go to war. He knew because they had let the other messengers escape. They had broken into tumult instead of action. He discerned fright in that tumult. He heard voices asking: 'Why did he do it?'

He wiped his matchet on the sand and went away. (p. 184.)

Okonkwo's suicide is reported off-stage. The tragic pattern is complete, his shame is absolute. There is, moreover, irony of a tragic kind at the end of the novel for Okonkwo in hanging himself, an abominated form of death, earns for himself a dishonourable burial like his father Unoka, the thing he had sought all his life to avoid. The hanging has been foreshadowed in comments throughout the novel. Okonkwo's first harvest was disastrous for all farmers and Achebe writes:

> That year the harvest was sad, like a funeral, and many farmers wept as they dug up the miserable and rotting yams. One man tied his cloth to a tree branch and hanged himself.
>
> (p. 22.)

Again, Uchendu in seeking to win Okonkwo from despair in his exile says that he himself has suffered much and adds, 'I did not hang myself, and I am still alive'. (p. 122.) This prepares the way for Okonkwo's death by hanging, his final act of despair. The symbolic pattern is complete. Obierika says to the District Commissioner to whom he appeals to cut down Okonkwo's body and bury it:

> It is an abomination for a man to take his own life. It is an offence against the Earth, and a man who commits it will not be buried by his clansmen. His body is evil, and only strangers may touch it. (p. 186.)

Okonkwo, 'one of the greatest men in Umuofia' is at the end totally alienated from his people and 'now he will be buried like a dog'. (p. 187.)

The final paragraph of the novel contains an irony of a different kind. Having embodied the tragic drama of a society in the tragic destiny of a representative member of that society, having suggested that the inexorable forces which determine Okonkwo's personal tragedy are analogous to the inevitable, irrepressible forces which determine historical change, Achebe seeks to distance himself from the particular events of the story and to fit both story and theme into a wider historical context. The dangling body of Okonkwo is merely an 'undignified detail' to the District Commissioner who has it cut down and the indifference displayed by him is symptomatic not only of the utter failure of the two systems to understand each other but, through the irony of the final paragraph, symptomatic of the hypocritical basis of the imperial-colonial notion of the 'civilizing mission', the idea contained in the phrase 'the white man's burden'.

The Commissioner went away, taking three of the four soldiers with him. In the many years in which he had toiled to bring civilisation to different parts of Africa he had learnt a number of things. One of them was that a District Commissioner must never attend to such undignified details as cutting down a hanged man from a tree. Such attention would give the natives a poor opinion of him. In the book which he planned to write he would stress that point. As he walked back to the court he thought about that book. Every day brought him some new material. The story of this man who had killed a messenger and hanged himself would make interesting reading. One could almost write a whole chapter on him. Perhaps not a whole chapter but a reasonable paragraph, at any rate. There was so much else to include, and one must be firm in cutting out details. He had already chosen the title of the book, after much thought: *The Pacification of the Primitive Tribes of the Lower Niger.* (p. 187.)

The novel is in fact a structure of ironies – irony of the tragic kind which shows an exceptional man see his best hopes and achievements destroyed through an inexorable flow of events which he is powerless to restrain, tragic irony suggested and supported by a carefully integrated pattern of minor ironies throughout the work – the accidental shooting which brings about his exile, the irony of the appeal of Christianity to Nwoye, Okonkwo's first born, in whom he placed his hopes, the irony contained in the persistent comment by Okonkwo that his daughter Ezinma ought to have been born a male child. And there is the more general irony made explicit in the closing paragraph of the book, but implicit in the encounter between the Africans and Europeans throughout the second and third parts, that Christianity, seen as a 'civilizing agent', acts as a catalyst in destroying a civilization which heretofore had strength and cohesion.

Things Fall Apart is the expression in terms of imaginative art of the tensions, stresses and conflicts, presented in personal, social and spiritual terms, of late nineteenth-century Ibo society. The men and women in the novel are real, they live in the world and seek to control their destinies, sometimes successfully, sometimes painfully and with difficulty and error. The inevitable processes of history are suggested by the struggle made concrete in the novel and conceived and presented in actual and particular terms, without idealism and without sentimentality.

No Longer at Ease

▼▼▼▼▼▼▼▼▼▼▼▼▼▼▼▼▼▼▼▼▼▼▼▼▼▼▼▼▼▼▼

OKONKWO takes his own life at the end of *Things Fall Apart* because he realizes that something critical to his existence has disappeared from his society and he refuses to live an alien in his own land. His action proceeds not from fear of punishment – he has twice endured that – and even the thought of death in payment for the murder of the white man's messenger is not what motivates him. His action proceeds rather from a profound sense of loss of values, and this time the loss, unlike that occasioned by his banishment of Mbaino, is irretrievable. Moreover, his action in killing himself is taken decisively and sums up the quality of his responses throughout the book. It reflects, in fact, the actions of the principal characters in the novel, all of whom act out of awareness of their situations – Nwoye adopts Christianity because it offers a way of life different to the way of life of his father, a life characterized by brutality; Obierika acts decisively in the series of situations he encounters: if he is a less tragic figure than Okonkwo it is because he is not of the same heroic disposition, though his awareness of the tragic situation of their society is as intense as that of his friend. The British administration acts decisively, even if wrongheadedly, in punishing the villagers of Abame and in imprisoning the chiefs – Okonkwo among them – of Umuofia, to cite but two examples. The Ibo villagers in adopting and applying the new monetary methods which European trading practices promote act with decision. Furthermore, the failure of the Umuofians to support Okonkwo in his final confrontation with the messengers from the District Officer proceeds not from indecisiveness, which a superficial reading of the scene would perhaps suggest, but from their collective recognition and decision that it is better *not* to support him. The decisiveness of the action both collective and personal which the book dramatizes reveals that while the fact of foreign encroachment has changed, or has begun to change, the nature of traditional life, the full implications of this change, the ambiguities it was to promote, are not yet apparent or palpable.

The second novel, *No Longer at Ease*, reveals the extent of these changes, the extent to which things have fallen apart in the society. If one word can characterize the circumstances in which the characters in the book find themselves, it is 'ambiguous'. If we say that *Things Fall Apart* is a structure of ironies, then *No Longer at Ease* is a structure of 'ambiguities', ambiguities which promote irresoluteness, indecisiveness and, through these, failure. None of the central characters escapes failure. Moreover, in an important way, society is seen to have failed. Once again irony is the characteristic mode of the novel but here, and unlike *Things Fall Apart* where the irony is the kind one associates with Aristotelian tragedy, the irony is more modern in its application. This kind of irony, of which more will be said, is the principal support in Achebe's attempt at structuring a modern tragedy.

No Longer at Ease is set in modern Nigeria, in the days immediately before Independence. It has as its hero Obi Okonkwo, the grandson of the Okonkwo of *Things Fall Apart*, and son of Nwoye, now called Isaac. The novel opens with Obi on trial for accepting bribes when a civil servant, and the book takes the form of a long flashback. The effect of the flashback is to concentrate attention on the causes for Obi's conviction and the complexity of events, actions and decisions which lead up to it. The consequences of Obi's trial – his public shame and humiliation – are important and Achebe presents them in terms of tragedy, modern tragedy which he is at pains to define. But Obi's tragedy is only wholly meaningful, and its relationship to the public theme the book embodies when its causes are understood. In *Things Fall Apart* Achebe's interest is in the processes of history, in the inexorable flow of events – processes which once initiated cannot be arrested – which overtake the whole of society and the central character who epitomizes its values. The destructive consequences are suggested in broad outlines – the old ways have changed, the traditional values have been turned upside-down. But the full consequences of the coming of Europeans is not yet known. Hints are given and the first novel offers a prophecy of what these changes will be in such passages as the following, already cited above, where Achebe writes that not only had the white man brought a 'lunatic religion' but 'he had also built a trading store and for the first time palm-oil and kernel became things of great price, and much money flowed into Umuofia'.

No Longer at Ease shows the nature and extent of the changes wrought by colonial intervention in Nigeria as they are revealed in the career of Obi, a character intensely individualized yet nevertheless representative of the young and educated Nigerian at this point in time. Obi is a modern man and his story comprises a modern tragedy. In this novel Achebe provides a record, transmuted by his personality and personal vision of, on the one hand, the nature of 'modernity' – in terms of its social, political and economic implications – imposed through colonial action on Nigeria, and, on the other, the price Nigerians have paid for it.

The main action of the novel begins with Obi's return from England where he recently completed his B.A. degree. Filled with idealism, Obi is determined to rid his country of corruption and to create a new and better nation. A second and related story concerns Obi's affair with Clara, a nurse whom he meets on the boat returning them to Nigeria and with whom he falls in love. Clara is *osu*, a descendant of slaves within the Ibo community and she, according to tradition, must live apart from the free-born.

The novel records Obi's professional, social and moral decline. He begins well enough, however. He is appointed Scholarship Secretary at the Federal Ministry of Education presided over by Mr Green, an Englishman of long standing in the Nigerian Colonial Service. Obi resists attempts at bribing him. The relationship with Clara at first is a happy one, despite the disapproval his friends and countrymen show and the warnings they offer. But a series of conflicting and simultaneous demands are made on Obi which undermine his security and eventually his integrity. The Lagos branch of the Umuofia Progressive Union which has paid for his education overseas expect Obi to repay the eight hundred pounds they have advanced him while at the same time to display a standard of living appropriate to his 'European' rank. This places a heavy burden on Obi's finances. As well as repaying the loan Obi feels obliged to purchase an expensive automobile, to lease and furnish an expensive flat in Ikoyi, and to send money home to pay for the education of his brothers. Moreover, he fails to win the approval of his parents when he speaks to them of his desire to marry Clara. As a result he tells her that they must delay their marriage and she, now pregnant by him, submits to a dangerous abortion and then leaves him, never to return.

Now demoralized, Obi succumbs to the many temptations around him, accepts bribes, reduces his debts and, at the precise moment he decides, because of his troubled conscience, to reform his ways is arrested and sent to trial, the outcome of which is shown in the opening passages of the novel.

At one level the novel reveals the wide gulf which exists between Obi's idealism based on his western education, and the relevance of this to his status as an individual within a complex and contradictory society in which many of the old values are still operative. Obi's ambiguous position is merely a reflection of the contradictions which inform society. Obi is able to articulate the ambiguities of his position and determine his conduct, both personal and professional, on the basis of the distinctions he is able to draw. At first he differs from those around him who either do not recognize inconsistencies in their behaviour as predicted by the clash between the old and the new, or, if they do, are not concerned to evaluate these inconsistencies, nor relate them to their personal behaviour.

Two elements of the story – Obi's dealings with the Umuofia Progressive Union and with his parents – point the certainty with which Achebe establishes the clash between traditional and modern values. The members of the U.P.U. are proud of Obi's success in winning a European education and are prepared to excuse him on the occasions when his behaviour does not conform with their opinion of how a 'been to' Nigerian ought to conduct himself – for example, his refusal to dress with the formality of Mr Udom (bowler hat, spats, and rolled umbrella) who has travelled with him on the boat; his refusal to use 'impressive' and stilted English which was much admired. Yet while they aspire to see Obi a modern man, in one sense the most modern – because the most influential – among them, they also expect him to honour custom and tradition. They are shocked by his affair with the *osu* Clara. This apparent contradiction in attitude is consolidated in the reaction of Obi's parents to his relationship with Clara. His father had rejected the ways of his father, Okonkwo, because of their inflexibility and brutality, epitomized in the death of Ikemefuna, and replaced them with the notion of Christian charity. When Obi points out the inconsistency between Christian belief and *osu* taboo held by his father, Isaac replies:

'I know Josiah Okeke very well.' He was looking steadily in front of him. His voice sounded tired. 'I know him and I know his wife. He is a good man and a great Christian. But he is *osu*. Naaman, captain of the host of Syria, was a great man and honourable, he was also a mighty man of valour, but he was a leper.' He paused so that this great and felicitous analogy might sink in with all its heavy and dreadful weight.

'*Osu* is like leprosy in the minds of our people. I beg of you, my son, not to bring the mark of shame and of leprosy into your family. If you do, your children and your children's children unto the third and fourth generations will curse your memory. It is not for myself I speak; my days are few. You will bring sorrow on your head and on the heads of your children. Who will marry your daughters? Whose daughters will your sons marry? Think of that, my son. We are Christians, but we cannot marry our own daughters.'*

Obi's mother whom he loves and to whom he looks for support, says:

'I did not tell anybody about that dream in the morning. I carried it in my heart wondering what it was. I took down my Bible and read the portion for the day. It gave me some strength, but my heart was still not at rest. In the afternoon your father came in with a letter from Joseph to tell us that you were going to marry an *osu*. I saw the meaning of my death in the dream. Then I told your father about it.' She stopped and took a deep breath. 'I have nothing to tell you in this matter except one thing. If you want to marry this girl, you must wait until I am no more. If God hears my prayers, you will not wait long.' She stopped again. Obi was terrified by the change that had come over her. She looked strange as if she had suddenly gone off her head.

*Achebe, Chinua, *No Longer at Ease*, Heinemann Educational Books 1963, pp. 133–4. All future page references in this chapter to this edition. Numbers correspond in the cased edition by William Heinemann 1960.

'Mother!' he called, as if she was going away. She held up her hand for silence.

'But if you do the thing while I am alive, you will have my blood on your head, because I shall kill myself.' She sank down completely exhausted. (pp. 135–6.)

The climax of the novel is effectively reached at this point. Obi's moral resolution, capable of resisting the pressures to which he is subjected in his professional life, cannot withstand the more powerful conviction of his mother. He repudiates Clara. His statement to her that they must postpone their marriage is mere rationalization. Shortly after this his mother dies and, paradoxically, his 'European' morality with her. He begins to take bribes and becomes like those around him whom he formerly despised. He has exchanged one kind of modern morality for another. His attempts to draw distinctions between accepting bribes from those candidates who are qualified and would likely win scholarships, and those who would not, is also mere rationalization.

The themes of individual morality and public responsibility are brought together at this point in the novel. Because of the collapse of his moral fibre, of which more will be said shortly, Obi accedes to pressures which have been placed on him from the outset. One of the important ironies of the novel lies in the fact that Obi's western education and the moral standard he derives from it render him incapable not only of standing against the traditional and conservative beliefs of his parents and their generation, but of existing effectively in 'modern' Nigeria. Obi's idealism, his moral standards, are those which Achebe, implicitly, recommends, although nowhere is any overt didactic purpose evident. Obi is a tragic figure and his tragedy proceeds from his modernity. He is, it is important to note, a victim of the same historical circumstances which overwhelmed his grandfather, the fact of colonialism.

Achebe has woven such an intricately patterned plot, has forged such unity in his treatment of the complexity of issues, both private and public, which determines Obi's actions that it violates the novel to separate them in an artificial manner. Yet this is necessary if we are to see not only how the artist works, but also how Achebe develops the theme of colonialism introduced in the first novel. Various passages in *No Longer at Ease*, of which the one cited below is typical, reveal the continuity of this theme in the two books and make clear that colonialism – the presence of Europe in Africa – is held to account for the change which has taken place in African society and for its present lack of moral centre. When Obi first meets his father and other members of the latter's age-group on his return from England, old Odogwu makes the following statement:

'He is the grandson of Ogbuefi Okonkwo who faced the white man single-handed and died in the fight. Stand up!' Obi stood up obediently.

'Remark him,' said Odogwu. 'He is Ogbuefi Okonkwo come back. He is Okonkwo *kpom-kwem*, exact, perfect.'

'Iguedo breeds great men,' said Odogwu changing the subject. 'When I was young I knew of them – Okonkwo, Ezeudu, Obierika, Okolo, Nwosu.' He counted them off with his right fingers against the left. 'And many others, as many as grains of sand. Among their fathers we hear of Ndu, Nwosisi, Ikedi, Obika and his brother Iweka – all giants. These men were great in their day. Today greatness has changed its tune. Titles are no longer great, neither are barns or large numbers of wives and children. Greatness is now in the things of the white man. And so we too have changed our tune. We are the first in all the nine villages to send our son to the white man's land.' (pp. 53–4.)

Obi is compared with his grandfather Okonkwo (although, ironically, in terms of the resolution of the novel and the qualities Obi displays at that time, a comparison with Okonkwo's father, Unoka, might be more fitting) and Obi is as much the victim of colonialism as was his grandfather. Moreover, through most of the novel Obi stands apart from society and its values in a way similar to Okonkwo at the end of *Things Fall Apart*. There are, of course, important differences in Achebe's presentation of Obi's final position which in no way resembles that of his forebear and these must be taken into account. There are oblique and subtle references to this, imbedded in the fabric of the novel, such as in the following passage. Obi is returning to Umuofia after his return from England and some of the passengers in the lorry by which he travels sing the following song:

'An in-law went to see his in-law
Oyiemu-o
His in-law seized him and killed him
Oyiemu-o
Bring a canoe, bring a paddle
Oyiemu-o
The paddle speaks English
Oyiemu-o.'

On the face of it there was no kind of logic or meaning in the
song. But as Obi turned it round and round in his mind, he
was struck by the wealth of association that even such a mediocre song could have. First of all it was unheard of for a man
to seize his in-law and kill him. To the Ibo mind it was the height
of treachery. Did not the elders say that a man's in-law was his
chi, his personal god? Set against this was another great
betrayal; a paddle that begins suddenly to talk in a language
which its master, the fisherman, does not understand. In
short then, thought Obi, the burden of the song was 'the world
turned upside down'. (p. 46.)

There is, as well, the incident, comic in conception, which described a village schoolmaster's reaction to a misplaced show of
white authority.

Mr Jones was the Inspector of Schools and was feared
throughout the province. It was said that he had fought
during the Kaiser's war and that it had gone to his head. He
was a huge man, over six feet tall. He rode a motor-cycle
which he always left about half a mile away so that he could
enter a school unannounced. Then he was sure to catch
somebody committing an offence. . . .
Now it was the headmaster who got into trouble. Obi never
discovered what the trouble was because it had all been done
in English. Mr Jones was red with fury as he paced up and
down, taking such ample strides that at one point Obi thought
he was making straight for him. The headmaster, Mr Nduka,
was all the while trying to explain something.
'Shut up!' roared Mr Jones, and followed it up with a
slap. Simeon Nduka was one of those people who had taken to

the ways of the white man rather late in life. And one of the things he had learnt in his youth was the great art of wrestling. In the twinkling of an eye Mr Jones was flat on the floor and the school was thrown into confusion. Without knowing why, teacher and pupils all took to their heels. To throw a white man was like unmasking an ancestral spirit. (pp. 64–5.)

What is important is that *No Longer at Ease* is, at one level, an exploration and elaboration of the theme of acquisitiveness which is introduced into the final section of *Things Fall Apart* and accounts for the resolution of that novel. The theme of corruption is the central theme of *No Longer at Ease* and corruption proceeds from the acquisitiveness which the forces of colonialism released in Ibo society. Corruption is the logical extension of acquisitiveness. This is the domination of the 'male' principle. The desire to acquire legitimate gain through trade is superseded by the desire to acquire money at any cost and through this, influence and power. Other themes are, of course, apparent but these relate to and elaborate the theme of acquisitiveness which is the core of the novel and accounts for the contradictions in Obi's behaviour, the ambiguous position in which he finds himself and for the uncertainty of his relations with the other characters. We do well to note that Achebe is concerned here, as in his earlier book, with changes wrought within Ibo society. It is through the beliefs and activities of the Lagos branch of the Umuofia Progressive Union that contemporary social acceptances are revealed and by them that much of the pressure which breaks Obi is placed. It is to Umuofia that Obi returns to seek important sanctions from his parents and when these are not forthcoming that he collapses. One hastens to add that this is not a novel solely about Ibo involvement in contemporary (i.e. late 1950) Nigerian life. References are made both to Europeans and to other Nigerian groups who are involved in the complex web of cause and effect which shape the destiny of the country and determine the morality of men like Obi. It is simply that Achebe approaches his material through a consideration of the beliefs, attitudes and values of the people he knows best and the implications of what has happened and is happening to that society in general terms proceeds from his specific renderings.

The theme of public corruption is suggested in the opening

c

pages of the novel in a comment innocent enough in itself but suggestive of the casual way in which corruption is taken for granted:

> Every available space in the court-room was taken up.
> There were almost as many people standing as sitting. The
> case had been the talk of Lagos for a number of weeks and on
> this last day anyone who could possibly leave his job was there
> to hear the judgement. Some Civil Servants paid as much as
> ten shillings and sixpence to obtain a doctor's certificate of ill-
> ness for the day. (pp. 1–2.)

Irony is apparent here. Public interest in Obi's case is high because he has been caught out. The courtroom is packed. The means by which people have found a place in the courtroom are similar in kind though different in degree to those employed by Obi. The atmosphere of corruption in public and private affairs, established early in the novel, is sustained throughout. Mr Green, Obi's boss in the Civil Service and a representative European voice, dismisses any sympathy for Obi by saying, categorically, 'The African is corrupt through and through'. Yet we are told by the members of the Lagos branch of the Umuofia Progressive Union that 'white men eat bribe' as well as Nigerians. 'Come to our Department. They eat more than black men nowadays.' (p. 33.) Before he has left the ship which returns him from England Obi is confronted with the pervasive custom of offering and accepting bribes:

> A young man, almost a boy in fact, was dealing with Obi's
> cabin. He told him that the duty on his radiogram would be
> five pounds.
> 'Right,' said Obi, feeling his hip-pockets. 'Write a receipt for
> me.' The boy did not write. He looked at Obi for a few seconds
> and then said: 'I can be able to reduce it to two pounds for
> you.'
> 'How?' asked Obi.
> 'I fit do it, but you no go get Government receipt.'
> For a few seconds Obi was speechless. Then he merely said:
> 'Don't be silly. If there was a policeman here I would hand
> you over to him.' The boy fled from his cabin without another
> word. Obi found him later attending other passengers.
> 'Dear old Nigeria,' he said to himself as he waited for
> another official to come to his cabin. (pp. 30–1.)

At the board when he is interviewed for his Civil Service post Obi is asked: 'Why do you want a job in the Civil Service? So you can take bribes?' Obi replies with a mixture of anger and contempt, that he would hardly admit it even if it were the case. There is a double irony in the scene, placed as it is in the book after Obi's trial when he is convicted of taking bribes, yet anticipating his career in the Civil Service at a time when he seeks to reform conditions to which he will ultimately fall victim. Yet, later, on his first trip to Umuofia the driver of the lorry 'dashes' a policeman as a means of having his certificate of 'road wordiness' accepted. Obi, appalled at the complicity of the police in the affair, is scorned by the driver and his fellow passengers:

. . . the driver's mate was approaching the other policeman. But just as he was about to hand something over to him Obi looked in their direction. The policeman was not prepared to take a risk; for all he knew Obi might be a C.I.D. man. So he drove the driver's mate away with great moral indignation. 'What do you want here? Go away!' Meanwhile the other policeman had found fault with the driver's papers and was taking down his particulars, the driver pleading and begging in vain. Finally he drove away, or so it appeared. About a quarter of a mile farther up the road he stopped.

'Why you look the man for face when we want give um him two shillings?' he asked Obi.

'Because he has no right to take two shillings from you,' Obi answered. . . .

It was only some minutes later that Obi realized why they had stopped. The driver's mate had run back to the policemen, knowing that they would be more amenable when there were no embarrassing strangers gazing at them. The man soon returned panting from much running.

'How much they take?' asked the driver.

'Ten shillings,' gasped his assistant.

'You see now,' he said to Obi, who was already beginning to feel a little guilty, especially as all the traders behind, having learnt what was happening, had switched their attacks from career girls to 'too know' young men. (pp. 42–3.)

Bribery, graft and corruption are endemic and the complexity of the situation as it obtains in Obi's Lagos arenowherebetter summed up than in the following passage:

> [Obi] had won his first battle hands-down. Everyone said it was impossible to win. They said a man expects you to accept 'kola' from him for services rendered, and until you do, his mind is never at rest. He feels like the inexperienced kite that carried away a duckling and was ordered by its mother to return it because the duck had said nothing, made no noise, just walked away. 'There is some grave danger in that kind of silence. Go and get a chick. We know the hen. She shouts and curses, and the matter ends there.' A man to whom you do a favour will not understand if you say nothing, make no noise, just walk away. You may cause more trouble by refusing a bribe than by accepting it. Had not a Minister of State said, albeit in an unguarded, alcoholic moment, that the trouble was not in receiving bribes, but in failing to do the thing for which the bribe was given? And if you refuse, how do you know that a 'brother' or a 'friend' is not receiving on your behalf, having told everyone that he is your agent? (pp. 87–8.)

Obi returns to Nigeria, the first Umuofian to win a degree and with it an important Civil Service post, determined to work towards ridding his country of corruption of this kind. He pins faith on the intellectual insights he has gained through his western education to support his strongly defined moral sense. He draws a distinction between the position of the established Civil Service and members of the new élite, of which he is representative, and shows how the latter may avoid the errors and pressures to which the former were subjected. Obi's convictions are revealed in conversation with his friend Christopher:

> . . . Obi and Christopher theorised about bribery in Nigeria's public life. Whenever Obi and Christopher met they were bound to argue very heatedly about Nigeria's future. Whichever line Obi took, Christopher had to take the opposite. Christopher was an economist from the London School of Economics and he always pointed out that Obi's arguments were not based on factual or scientific analysis, which was not surprising since he had taken a degree in English.

'The Civil Service is corrupt because of these so-called experienced men at the top,' said Obi.

'You don't believe in experience? You think that a chap straight from university should be made a permanent secretary?'

'I didn't say straight from the university, but even that would be better than filling our top posts with old men who have no intellectual foundations to support their experience.'

'What about the Land Officer jailed last year? He is straight from the university.'

'He is an exception,' said Obi. 'But take one of these old men. He probably left school thirty years ago in Standard Six. He has worked steadily to the top through bribery – an ordeal by bribery. To him the bribe is natural. He gave it and he expects it. Our people say that if you pay homage to the man on top, others will pay homage to you when it is your turn to be on top. Well, that is what the old men say.'

'What do the young men say, if I may ask?'

'To most of them bribery is no problem. They come straight to the top without bribing anyone. It's not that they're necessarily better than others, it's simply that they can afford to be virtuous. But even that kind of virtue can become a habit.' (pp. 20–1.)

Irony is apparent here, too, since Obi in his own mind, one of those who can afford to be virtuous, is proven wrong as the subsequent action of the book reveals. In another conversation with Christopher later in the book the moral climate of the country is displayed with Christopher's attitudes, to which Obi stands diametrically opposed, representing the general moral acceptances which obtain. Here Obi tells his friend the story of Miss Marks, who attempted to influence Obi first through her brother, who offered Obi money, and then on her own behalf when she offered Obi herself. The conversation proceeds with Christopher saying:

'What happened to her in the end?'

'Oh, she is in England. She got the scholarship all right.'

'You are the biggest ass in Nigeria,' said Christopher, and they began a long argument on the nature of bribery.

'If a girl offers to sleep with you, that is not bribery,' said Christopher.

'Don't be silly,' replied Obi. 'You mean you honestly cannot see anything wrong in taking advantage of a young girl straight from school who wants to go to a university?'

'Don't imagine that girls are angels.'

'I was not imagining any such thing. But it is scandalous that a man of your education can see nothing wrong in going to bed with a girl before you let her appear before the board.'

'This girl was appearing before the board, anyway. That was all she expected you to do: to see that she did appear. And how do you know she did not go to bed with the board members?'

'She probably did.'

'Well then, what good have you done her?'

'Very little, I admit,' said Obi, trying to put his thoughts in order, 'but perhaps she will remember that there was one man at least who did not take advantage of his position . . .'

'Now tell me, Christopher. What is *your* definition of bribery?'

'Well, let's see. . . . The use of improper influence.'

'Good. I suppose —

'But the point is, there was no influence at all. The girl was going to be interviewed, anyway. She came voluntarily to have a good time. I cannot see that bribery is involved at all.'

'Of course, I know you're not really serious.'

'I am dead serious.'

'But I'm surprised you cannot see that the same argument can be used for taking money. If the applicant is getting the job, anyway, then there is no harm in accepting money from him.'

'Well —

'Well, what?'

'You see, the difference is this.' He paused. 'Let's put it this way. No man wants to part with his money. If you accept money from a man you make him poorer. But if you go to bed with a girl who asks for it, I don't see that you have done any harm.' (pp. 120–1.)

The important thing to note here is not only Obi's attitudes and convictions as revealed in the discussion, but also the elaborate, hair-splitting and unconvincing rationalizations which are offered to excuse acceptance of the debased morality of the moment. And at the end of the trial, when Obi has been found guilty of accepting bribes, he is condemned by the Umuofia Progressive Union not because he has accepted them, but because he was caught.

> The President said it was a thing of shame for a man in the senior service to go to prison for twenty pounds. He repeated twenty pounds, spitting it out. 'I am against people reaping where they have not sown. But we have a saying that if you want to eat a toad you should look for a fat and juicy one.'
> 'It is all lack of experience,' said another man. 'He should not have accepted the money himself. What others do is tell you to go and hand it to their houseboy. Obi tried to do what everyone does without finding out how it was done.' He told the proverb of the house rat who went swimming with his friend the lizard and died from cold, for while the lizard's scales kept him dry the rat's hairy body remained wet. (p. 6.)

Yet it would seem to be Achebe's contention that it is through the actions of the new élite that reform will have to come if it is to come at all. Obi dismisses perhaps too casually and, perhaps this is a weakness in the structure of the novel, a variety of alternatives to the solution he proposes:

> 'Where does one begin? With the masses? Educate the masses?' He shook his head. 'Not a chance there. It would take centuries. A handful of men at the top. Or even one man with vision – an enlightened dictator. People are scared of the word nowadays. But what kind of democracy can exist side by side with so much corruption and ignorance? Perhaps a half-way house – a sort of compromise.' When Obi's reasoning reached this point he reminded himself that England had been as corrupt not so very long ago. He was not really in the mood for consecutive reasoning. His mind was impatient to roam in a more pleasant landscape. (pp. 43–4.)

The passage is important not only because it suggests the alternatives open to a country by which it may achieve its goals at the time it achieves independence, but also because it reveals part of the reason for Obi's failure to realise his ideals. At critical moments Obi is either not prepared or not able to engage in 'consecutive reasoning'. 'His mind was impatient to roam in a more pleasant atmosphere.' (How like his great grandfather Unoka). By the time he gets down to serious self-scrutiny – when he is rejected by his mother, when he has lost Clara and when his career and his idealism are in jeopardy – it is too late to mend: 'His mind was troubled not only by what had happened but also by the discovery that there was nothing in him with which to challenge it honestly.' (p. 137.)

The core of the novel is the moral dilemma in which Obi finds himself and the conflict in the novel is produced by the clash between the strength of his moral awareness on the one hand and his almost total lack of moral courage in sustaining it. His ideal of right conduct in his job is morally sound. While it may be naïve and not take into full account the practical realities of the public, political situation, it is at least personally viable and could prevail if his moral strength were sufficient. Similarly, in the case of Clara he knows that the caste system which makes Clara unsuitable as a wife is irrational. What is required of him in this instance is a strong show of moral courage to support his intellectual assessment of the situation. This courage Obi seems to possess as is revealed in his dealings with the Umuofia Progressive Union who castigate him for his involvement with Clara, but especially in the scene with Joseph, his townsman, which not only shows the fairness of Obi's evaluation of Clara's position, but also reveals the ambiguous position in which his western education has placed him so far as his peers are concerned.

> 'Look at me,' said Joseph, getting up and tying his coverlet as a loincloth. He now spoke in English. 'You know book, but this is no matter for book. Do you know what an *osu* is? But how can you know?' In that short question he said in effect that Obi's mission-house upbringing and European education had made him a stranger in his country – the most painful thing one could say to Obi.

'I know more about it than yourself,' he said, 'and I'm going to marry the girl. I wasn't actually seeking your approval.'

Joseph thought the best thing was to drop the matter for the present. He went back to bed and was soon snoring.

Obi felt better and more confident in his decision now that there was an opponent, the first of hundreds to come no doubt. Perhaps it was not a decision really; for him there could be only one choice. It was scandalous that in the middle of the twentieth century a man could be barred from marrying a girl simply because her great-great-great-great-grandfather had been dedicated to serve a god, thereby setting himself apart and turning his descendants into a forbidden caste to the end of Time. Quite unbelievable. And here was an educated man telling Obi he did not understand. 'Not even my mother can stop me,' he said as he lay down beside Joseph. (pp. 71–2.)

But he vacillates at critical moments. When his mother says she will kill herself if he marries Clara, sheer terror replaces moral resolve and the rationalization process which is to prove his undoing begins. All this is made quite plain at the time Clara is taken away by the doctor who will perform the abortion which almost costs her her life: 'Obi wanted to rush out of his car and shout: "Stop, let's go and get married now," but he couldn't and didn't.' (p. 149.) Clara's leaving him, the death of his mother, and more financial demands leave him dispirited and inert. Now in neither his private life nor his public affairs can he, at critical moments, display the courage, make the stand required of him. Consequently his interests suffer and he loses all.

Another important consideration is that Obi's tragedy arises in part from his well-meaningness. This may well be interpreted as moral lassitude but at least his actions do not proceed, as do those of most of the characters in the novel apart from Clara, from selfishness. One of the principal ironies of the novel is centred in this; that Obi in seeking to please everyone pleases no one and further that no one understands for a moment the source and motive of his actions. The novel closes with the following paragraph:

Everybody wondered why. The learned judge, as we have

seen, could not comprehend how an educated young man
and so on and so forth. The British Council man, even the men
of Umuofia, did not know. And we must presume that, in spite
of his certitude, Mr Green did not know either. (p. 170.)

We have seen above the reactions of the men of Umuofia. Mr
Green, a man who despises the educated African and who claims
to understand the circumstances in which Obi finds himself offers
the following reasons to account for the failure of men like Obi:

> 'What facts?' asked the British Council man, who was
> relatively new to the country. There was a lull in the general
> conversation, as many people were now listening to Mr Green
> without appearing to do so.
> 'The fact that over countless centuries the African has
> been the victim of the worst climate in the world and of every
> imaginable disease. Hardly his fault. But he has been sapped
> mentally and physically. We have brought him Western
> education. But what use is it to him? He is. . . .' (p. 3.)

The reasons he offers show his utter inability to comprehend the
plight of Obi and reveals out-of-date paternalist attitudes of the
colonial period. That this is so is communicated to us in the passage
where Obi muses on the reasons for Mr Green's tireless devotion
in his job to a people he despises:

> He must have come originally with an ideal – to bring light
> to the heart of darkness, to tribal head-hunters performing
> weird ceremonies and unspeakable rites. But when he arrived,
> Africa played him false. Where was his beloved bush full
> of human sacrifice? There was St George horsed and capari-
> soned, but where was the dragon? In 1900 Mr Green might
> have ranked among the great missionaries; in 1935 he would
> have made do with slapping headmasters in the presence of
> their pupils; but in 1957 he could only curse and swear.
> With a flash of insight Obi remembered his Conrad which
> he had read for his degree. 'By the simple exercise of our will
> we can exert a power for good practically unbounded.' That
> was Mr Kurtz before the heart of darkness got him. After-
> wards he had written: 'Exterminate all the brutes.' It was not a
> close analogy, of course. Kurtz had succumbed to the dark-

ness, Green to the incipient dawn. But their beginning and
their end were alike. (p. 106.)

The questions posed by the final paragraph of the novel are
rhetorical: the novel has offered, implicitly and in dramatic form,
the answers to them.

It is important to note as well that Obi's sense of moral right re-
asserts itself, ironically, when it is too late to do him any good. His
decision to reform almost at the precise moment that he is caught
may appear as rather too self-conscious plotting on Achebe's part
as a device to underline a conviction that evil is to be punished.
This is too facile an interpretation for clearly Obi's guilt is as
nothing when compared with that of society: he is punished for his
offence and society goes its untrammelled way. The event indicates rather the consistency of Achebe's approach to his theme by
pointing up the morality, both public and private, which he
recommends:

> In due course he paid off his bank overdraft and his debt
> to the Hon. Sam Okoli, M.H.R. The worst was now over, and
> Obi ought to have felt happier. But he didn't.
> Then one day someone brought twenty pounds. As the
> man left, Obi realised that he could stand it no more. People
> say that one gets used to these things, but he had not found it
> like that at all. Every incident had been a hundred times
> worse than the one before it. (p. 169.)

Seen in this context the statement that 'there was nothing in him
with which to challenge his problems' becomes ambiguous.

It is not, then, simply a matter of Obi's moral weakness though
this is an important part of it. Obi can see no way out of his problems, out of the ambiguous moral and social position in which he
finds himself, because at this point in time – this is Achebe's point
and this is how he achieves a tragic vision not only of an individual
but of society – there is *no* way out for a man of Obi's nature,
character and resolve. It is from this recognition that the general-
ized application of the novel is revealed. Achebe makes it clear that
Obi is a modern Nigerian pulled between two sets of values, those
modern and those traditional. This is emphasized throughout the
novel but two passages will serve to make the point clearly. The

first records a conversation between Obi and Christopher, the latter throughout the novel a foil to Obi:

> 'You know, Obi,' he said, 'I had wanted to discuss that matter with you. But I have learnt not to interfere in a matter between a man and a woman, especially with chaps like you who have wonderful ideas about love. A friend came to me last year and asked my advice about a girl he wanted to marry. I knew this girl very very well. She is, you know, very liberal. So I told my friend: 'You shouldn't marry this girl.' Do you know what this bloody fool did? He went and told the girl what I said. That was why I didn't tell you anything about Clara. You may say that I am not broad-minded, but I don't think we have reached the stage where we can ignore all our customs. You may talk about education and so on, but I am not going to marry an *osu*.' (pp. 143–4.)

The second and more important is an exchange between Obi and Joseph over the matter of Clara (note the effect gained through the ambiguity implied by the use of the word 'pioneer'):

> 'Look at me, Obi.' Joseph invariably asked people to look at him. 'What you are going to do concerns not only yourself but your whole family and future generations. If one finger brings oil it soils the others. In future, when we are all civilised, anybody may marry anybody. But that time has not come. We of this generation are only pioneers.'
> 'What is a pioneer? Someone who shows the way. That is what I am doing. Anyway, it is too late to change now.'
> 'It is not,' said Joseph. . . . 'It is not too late to change. Remember you are the one and only Umuofia son to be educated overseas. We do not want to be like the unfortunate child who grows his first tooth and grows a decayed one. What sort of encouragement will your action give to the poor men and women who collected the money? (p. 75.)

Obi's intelligence, honed by his western education, caused him at first to view objectively situations which ultimately engage his emotional responses. It is the latter which prevail at critical times. When in a moment of introspection he realizes he has not the moral stamina to deal with his problems, more than simply self-appraisal is offered. Appraisal of the circumstances in which any young man like Obi will find themselves – influenced by an idealism which seeks to achieve honesty and success in public and private affairs and this in contention with out-worn values which nevertheless still have force – is implied. In this connection the appropriateness of the quotation from T. S. Eliot from which the title of the novel is taken is apparent:

> We returned to our places, these kingdoms,
> But no longer at ease here, in the old dispensation,
> With an alien people clutching their gods.
> I should be glad of another death.

Achebe conceives the story in tragic terms, but tragedy of a particularly modern kind. There is an element of the *roman a thèse* in the novel which proceeds not from Achebe's attempt to create a modern tragedy, but from the need he seems to have felt to define what he is going to attempt and then deliberately to illustrate this. At his interview for appointment to a Civil Service post the following discussion takes place between Obi and the Chairman:

> 'You say you're a great admirer of Graham Greene. What do you think of *The Heart of the Matter*?'
> 'The only sensible novel any European has written on West Africa and one of the best novels I have read.' Obi paused, and then added almost as an afterthought: 'Only it was nearly ruined by the happy ending.'
> The Chairman sat up in his chair.
> 'Happy ending? Are you sure it's *The Heart of the Matter* you're thinking about? The European police officer commits suicide.'
> 'Perhaps happy ending is too strong, but there is no other way I can put it. The police officer is torn between his love of a woman and his love of God, and he commits suicide. It's much too simple. Tragedy isn't like that at all. I remember an old man in my village, a Christian convert, who suffered one calamity after another. He said life was like a bowl of wormwood which one sips a little at a time world without end. He understood the nature of tragedy.'
> 'You think that suicide ruins a tragedy,' said the Chairman.

'Yes. Real tragedy is never resolved. It goes on hopelessly
for ever. Conventional tragedy is too easy. The hero dies
and we feel a purging of the emotions. A real tragedy takes
place in a corner, in an untidy spot, to quote W. H. Auden.
The rest of the world is unaware of it.' (p. 39.)

This passage indicates a minor flaw in the novel and here Achebe
momentarily loses his objectivity and almost breaks the dramatic
pattern of the novel by obtruding himself between his book and
his reader. But the general application of the opinions offered in
the passage is clear enough. They imply Achebe's recognition that
heroic tragic response of the kind made by Okonkwo is no longer
possible. Those of Okonkwo imply a fixed society or a society at
the point where irrevocable change is about to take place, change
recognized by a character who is the epitome of that society who
dies and in whose death is symbolized the death of the old ways.
Modern Nigerian life, on the other hand, with its accelerated
pace of social change producing instability in the society and in
the individuals who comprise it will produce tragedy of the kind
Obi's life displays. Achebe's definition of modern tragedy arises
out of his estimate of the contemporary Nigerian scene. Here a
sense of the loss, the tragic waste of a man, on the whole a good
man, is revealed. But his tragedy is enacted in an 'untidy spot'
and the 'rest of the world is unaware of it'. Something of the same
kind of irony which informs the closing passage of *Things Fall
Apart* is apparent at the close of *No Longer at Ease*.

Yet Achebe's near intrusion into the pattern of his book does
not detract from its excellence. It is like the first novel concrete yet
general, local yet universal, in presenting an individual whose
story is told dramatically within the pages of a carefully planned
and executed book. The language as in the first book is appropriate
to the themes and occasions of the book. When Obi speaks to the
chairman of the Civil Service board in the passage cited above, the
language is modern and colloquial. When, on the other hand, he is
addressed by the pastor Mr Ikeda as he is about to depart for
England, the language is couched in an idiom appropriate to the
clan and village:

Mr Ikedi . . . turned to the young man on his right. 'In times
past,' he told him, 'Umuofia would have required of you to

fight in her wars and bring home human heads. But those were
days of darkness from which we have been delivered by the
blood of the Lamb of God. Today we send you to bring
knowledge. Remember that the fear of the Lord is the beginning of wisdom. I have heard of young men from other towns
who went to the white man's country, but instead of facing
their studies they went after the sweet things of the flesh. Some
of them even married white women.' The crowd murmured its
strong disapproval of such behaviour. 'A man who does that is
lost to his people. He is like rain wasted in the forest. I would
have suggested getting you a wife before you leave. But the
time is too short now. Anyway, I know that we have no fear
where you are concerned. We are sending you to learn book.
Enjoyment can wait. Do not be in a hurry to rush into the
pleasures of the world like the young antelope who danced
herself lame when the main dance was yet to come.' (pp. 10–11.)

It is Achebe's intellectual understanding of his characters which
enables him to describe aspects of human character, and more
important, to describe successfully how a character develops. This
is rare among contemporary Nigerian writers. When they want to
show a good man changing to bad, for example, they cut him in
two as it were: they show a good man in the first part of their
book and a bad man in the latter half. Little is given to account for
the changes which take place. This is not the case with Achebe in
No Longer at Ease: he is careful to maintain in Obi those constant
characteristics which keeps him a recognizable individual. Obi
on his first appearance, once the proper action of the novel is got
going, is an enthusiastic and idealistic young Nigerian, intent on
serving his country through a highly idealized yet acceptable
moral code. At the end he is defeated: his idealism is destroyed and
he is the subject of popular interest not so much because he 'ate
bribe' but because he was caught. Achebe portrays the changes
through which Obi passes with considerable astuteness of observation. We see how the pressures on him in his private and public
life lower his spirits, reduce his moral strength and ultimately
cause him to put scruples aside. But however much he has altered
at the close of the book we see him as the same Obi whom we met
when the flashback section of the book began. Nor do we find the

changes in him inexplicable. For, from the start, we have been
aware of the weakness in his nature which in difficult circumstances
will render him impotent. Obi has not the moral strength to
match and support his intellectual strength. When his intellectual
decision about what is right – the need to thwart corruption and, in
the case of Clara, the need to stand against the *osu* tradition – are
challenged he has little to resist the challenge. The situations in
which Achebe places Obi are precisely those most likely to find
out his weakness: and he shows exactly and with economy the
ways in which Obi gives way to his weakness, vacillates and adjusts
his principles to suit his actions until ultimately he is transformed
to the man of the final pages of the novel.

Obi's experiences testify, in situations which are sometimes
comic, sometimes pathetic, sometimes grim, to the oppressive
weight of doubt, guilt, shame and regret that the colonial experience has imposed on modern Nigeria, particularly on young men
in the city where the effects of this history are most carefully
organized and acutely felt.

Arrow of God

ARROW OF GOD, Achebe's third novel, is the most ample of his books, the one in which he explores the two themes which dominate *Things Fall Apart* – the nature and quality of Ibo village life as a consideration in their own right, and the effects of colonialism on that life – at greater breadth and depth than in the first novel. As in the first book the forces of colonialism – church, government and trade – precipitate the crisis and tragic resolution in the novel which alters the quality of tribal life and destroys the hero of the book, a man who epitomizes that life.

Arrow of God is set in the period between *Things Fall Apart* and *No Longer at Ease*; that is, the period when colonialism had become entrenched in Nigeria. The locale is Umuaro and the other villages which form a union of six villages. Achebe presents the area as the centre of things and explains his motive in returning to an earlier setting than *No Longer at Ease* in this way:

> I think I'm basically an ancestor worshipper. . . . Not in the same sense as my grandfather would probably do it, you know, pouring palm wine on the floor for the ancestors. . . . With me it takes the form of celebration and I feel a certain compulsion to do this. It's not because I think this will appeal to my readers, but because I feel this is something that has to be done before I move on to the contemporary scene. And in fact the reason [*Arrow of God*] goes back to the past, not as remotely as the first [novel] is that I've learned to think that my first book is no longer adequate. I've learned a lot more about these particular people . . . my ancestors.[20]

This accounts for the density of the description of the complex tribal life the novel evokes. But it says nothing of the form in which the work is cast, a form like that of the first novel which is essentially dramatic. That is, Achebe is not merely describing the daily round of social and religious life in a representative community, as many modern Nigerian novels do. Rather he is showing this community under stress which in turn promotes change. As in *Things Fall Apart* the forces of colonialism, more powerful and irresistible, cause the change. The presence of the white man suggests a world outside that of Umuaro, but it is the power and influence of white men in shaping the day to day destinies of the Umuaro villagers which counts with them and on which Achebe focuses. As it turns out, though there is no evidence that this was Achebe's deliberate intention, *Arrow of God* becomes the central volume in a trilogy of novels in which Achebe explores the consequences of colonial rule in one area of Nigeria.

At the centre of the novel is Ezeulu, chief priest of Ulu, a god created at the time when the six villages banded together for protection against slave raids to supersede older village deities. One of the principal purposes of the novel, Achebe tells us, is to explore the nature of this kind of power:

> I'm handling a whole lot of . . . more complex themes, . . . like the relationship between a god and his priest. My chief character in this novel is a village priest not a Christian priest – a traditional African religion. And I'm interested in this old question of who decides what shall be the wish of the gods, and . . . that kind of situation.[21]

A powerful and forceful character, with nobility, Ezeulu in many ways resembles Okonkwo in *Things Fall Apart* but he experiences none of the inner doubts and uncertainties of the latter. Achebe accounts for his conception of the two characters in this way: speaking of the two novels and specifying that *Arrow of God* is not in any strict sense a continuation of *Things Fall Apart*, he says:

> It is the same area – the supporting background and scenery are the same – I'm writing about the same people. But the story itself is not – in fact I see it as the exact opposite. Ezeulu the chief character in *Arrow of God* is a different kind of man from Okonkwo. He is an intellectual. He thinks about why things happen – he is a priest and his office requires this – so he goes to the roots of things and he's ready to accept change, intellectually. He sees the value of change and therefore his

reaction to Europe is completely different from Okonkwo's. He is ready to come to terms with it – up to a point – except where his dignity is involved. This he could not accept; he's very proud. So you see it's really the other side of the coin, and the tragedy is that they come to the same sticky end.[22]

Achebe's indication of his intention as explained here provide a basis for judging the book and a point of view from which it may be judged: that is, here again the events are seen in terms of tragedy which elevate the book above a merely descriptive concern.

When we meet him first Ezeulu's power is supreme. Yet secure as his power and influence are, they need to be protected from outside pressures which threaten to undermine them. The tension in the novel proceeds from Ezeulu's defence of his god and himself, and to evoke this Achebe has constructed a complex yet unified dramatic treatment displaying a combination of events which lead to tragic consequences at both the individual and social levels. Against a carefully developed background describing Umuaro history through a series of births, deaths, marriages, celebrations, religious ceremonies Achebe displays the context in which Ezeulu lives and over which he presides, and displays the pressures brought to bear on him. The background, while the same as *Things Fall Apart*, is more elaborately established. A cursory reading of the novel suggests that much of the background is there for its own sake, that it has come to dominate the book and has in a sense become the subject of the book. There is much in the novel which has little direct relation to the story the novel has to tell. Yet the gains made in terms of the overall tragic consequences the novel displays wherein a whole society is involved are obvious once Achebe's purpose is taken into account.

Ezeulu is compelled to defend his unique position of priest of Ulu, the most powerful of the village deities against, on the one hand, reactionary forces within the tribe and, on the other, against European culture and religion. The former theme is centred in the rivalry between Ezeulu and Nwaka, a wealthy chief and principal supporter of Ezidemili, the chief priest of the god Idemili, one of the deities displaced by Ulu. This rivalry promotes internal division in the tribe. The second theme is symbolized in Ezeulu's relationship with Captain Winterbottom, the head of the local colonial political administration. The two themes are related. The older deities 'Idemili and Ogwugwu and Eru had never been happy with their secondary role since the villages got together and made Ulu and put him over the older deities.'* The most powerful of these rivals are Nwaka and Ezidemili and their antagonism is of long standing.

'Jealousy for what? I am not the first Ezeulu in Umuaro, he is not the first Ezidemili. If his father and his father's father and all the others before them were not jealous of my fathers why should he be of me? No, it is not jealousy but foolishness; the kind that puts its head into the pot. But if it is jealousy, let him go on. The fly that perches on a mound of dung may strut around as long as it likes, it cannot move the mound. (p. 161.)

This traditional rivalry is intensified by Ezeulu's stand against Nwaka and Ezidemili over a land dispute with a rival village. Umuaro had sent a representative to Okperi to claim land which the former believed to belong to them. The claim is disputed by Okperi and in heated argument the Umuaro representative commits blasphemy by destroying the image of the personal god of one of the Okperi. For this the Umuaro man loses his life. The elders of Umuaro call a council of war. Nwaka and Ezidemili call for war against Okperi to avenge their dead kinsman and gain the land to which they claim title. Ezeulu stands against them because he believes their claim to be spurious. He advises against fighting an unjust war. Nwaka and Ezidemili prevail and a war is started only to be brought to a sudden close by Winterbottom who thereby gains the name 'breaker of guns' among the Umuaro villagers. Ezeulu testifies before Winterbottom that the Okperi land did not belong to Umuaro and thus wins favour with the District Officer.

Ezeulu is prepared to exploit his friendship with Winterbottom because he sees not only that to resist would be pointless but that change is inevitable and gains can be made. He refers to what happened to Abame, and the reference suggests the continuity of Achebe's exploration of the theme he introduced in *Things Fall Apart*, and says:

* Achebe, Chinua, *Arrow of God*, Heinemann Educational Books 1965, p. 49. All further page references in this chapter are to this edition. Page numbers in cased edition by William Heinemann 1964 are the same.

'How many white men went in the party that destroyed Abame? Do you know? Five.' He held his right hand up with five fingers fanned out. 'Five. Now have you ever heard that five people – even if their heads reached the sky – could over-run a whole clan? Impossible. With all their power and magic white men would not have overrun entire Ulu and Igbo if we did not help them. Who showed them the way to Abame? They were not born there; how then did they find the way? We showed them and are still showing them. So let nobody come to me now and complain that the white man did this and did that. The man who brings ant-infested faggots into his hut should not grumble when lizards begin to pay him a visit.' (pp. 162–3.)

Given this set of circumstances, aware that to resist the white man is impossible and foolhardy, concerned to know as much as he can about the intention of the white man and the nature of his religion and to turn it to his own account, Ezeulu has sent his son Udoche to the mission school with this injunction:

'I want one of my sons to join these people and be my eye there. If there is nothing in it you will come back. But if there is something there you will bring home my share. The world is like a Mask dancing. If you want to see it well you do not stand in one place. My spirit tells me that those who do not befriend the white man today will be saying *had we known* tomorrow.' (p. 55.)

In connection with the first of these two passages is a statement which offers an ironic foreshadowing of the effects of Ezeulu's involvement with the white man, one which he could not calculate at the time but which is shrewdly posited by his great friend and confidant, Akuebue, who stands in relation to Ezeulu as Obierika did to Okonkwo in the first novel. To Ezeulu's question: 'When the clan chose to go to war with Okperi over a piece of land which did not belong to us . . . did I not stand up then and tell Umuaro what would happen;' (pp. 161–2.) Akuebue replies:

'I do not doubt that,' said Akuebue and, in a sudden access of impatience and recklessness, added, 'but you forget one thing: that no man however great can win judgement against a clan. You may think you did in that land dispute but you are wrong. Umuaro will always say that you betrayed them before the white man. And they will say that you are betraying them again today by sending your son to join in desecrating the land.' (p. 162.)

To which Ezeulu answers:

'We went to war against Okperi who are our blood brothers over a piece of land which did not belong to us and you blame the white man for stepping in. Have you not heard that when two brothers fight a stranger reaps their harvest?' (p. 162.)

Akuebue understands Ezeulu's motives, even while he offers a gloomy prophecy of where these will lead the priest, but Ezeulu's enemies see them as merely a more blatant manifestation of Eze- ulu's ambition and pride. Their antagonism increases when Udoche, the Christianized son, attempts to kill the sacred python of Idemili by placing it in his foot-locker. The symbolism here is clear enough: just as the python struggles for survival, so the old gods struggle against the new religion. Ezeulu's refusal to punish Udoche is seen as further evidence of Ezeulu's rapprochement with the white man and this is further enhanced in a speech by Nwaka at a meeting called by Ezeulu to tell that clan that he has been called before Winterbottom. Note the clever play on words which suggests how the presence and standards of the white man are generally regarded in Umuaro.

'The white man is Ezeulu's friend and has sent for him. What is so strange about that? He did not send for me. He did not send for Udeozo; he did not send for the priest of Idemili; he did not send for the priest of Eru; he did not send for the priest of Udo nor did he ask the priest of Ogwugwu to come and see him. He has asked Ezeulu. Why? Because they are friends. Or does Ezeulu think that their friendship should stop short of entering each other's houses? Does he want the white man to be his friend only by word of mouth? Did not our elders tell us that as soon as we shake hands with a leper he will want an embrace? It seems to me that Ezeulu has shaken hands with a man of white body.' This brought low murmurs of applause and even some laughter. Like many potent things from which people shrink in fear leprosy is nearly always called by its more polite and appeasing name – *white body*. . . .

'What I say is this,' continued Nwaka, 'a man who brings ant-ridden faggots into his hut should expect the visit of lizards. But if Ezeulu is now telling us that he is tired of the white man's friendship our advice to him should be: You tied the knot, you should also know how to undo it. You passed the shit that is smelling; you should carry it away. Fortunately the evil charm brought in at the end of a pole is not too difficult to take outside again.

'I have heard one or two voices murmuring that it is against custom for the priest of Ulu to travel far from his hut. I want to ask such people: Is this the first time Ezeulu would be going to Okperi? Who was the white man's witness that year we fought for our land – and lost?' He waited for the general murmuring to die down. 'My words are finished. I salute you all.' (pp. 177–8.)

The reference to the leper in Nwaka's speech echoes one made earlier and one similar in kind by Ezeulu regarding the new religion when he says: ' . . . the new religion was like a leper. Allow him a handshake and he wants an embrace.' (p. 5.)

Hard as Nwaka's words are, Ezeulu is less angered by them than by those of others who would compromise or seek to appease him:

As always his anger was not caused by open hostility such as Nwaka showed in his speech but by the sweet words of people like Nnabenyi. They looked to him like rats gnawing away at the sole of a sleeper's foot, biting and then blowing air on the wound to soothe it, and lull the victim back to sleep. (p. 179.)

Ezeulu has delayed his departure for Government Hill so that he might inform the clan that he has been summoned by Winterbottom lest they suspect his motives. In doing this Ezeulu incurs Winterbottom's anger and is put peremptorily in the guardhouse. Winterbottom, tired and ill, collapses in a coma and this is seen by the Umuaro community as Ezeulu's revenge on Winterbottom for the insult offered him. Winterbottom's action is typical of the errors in understanding and judgement committed by the colonial administration. The forces of colonialism are seen in this novel, as in *Things Fall Apart*, as disruptive and just as Achebe broadens and deepens his treatment of Ibo communal life so he expands his rendering of the influence of Europe. The continuity in theme between the two novels is apparent in different ways – in the reference to the punitive expedition sent into Abame on Okonkwo's time, in such phrases as 'before the white man turned us upside down', in the fact that a young A.D.O., Tony Clarke, is given *The Pacification of the Primitive Tribes of the Lower Niger*, a passage of which, Kiplinesque in tone, is cited.

[Clarke] had now had the book for over a fortnight and must finish and take it back this evening. One of the ways in which the tropics were affecting him was the speed of his reading. In any case the book was pretty dull. It was too smug for Clarke's taste. But he was now finding the last few paragraphs quite stirring. The chapter was headed THE CALL.

'For those seeking but a comfortable living and a quiet occupation Nigeria is closed and will be closed until the earth has lost some of its deadly fertility and until the people live under something like sanitary conditions. But for those in search of a strenuous life, for those who can deal with men as others deal with material, who can grasp great situations, coax events, shape destinies and ride on the crest of the wave of time Nigeria is holding out her hands. For the men who in India have made the Briton the law-maker, the organizer, the engineer of the world this new, old land has great rewards and honourable work. I know we can find the men. Our mothers do not draw us with nervous grip back to the fireside of boyhood, back into the home circle, back to the purposeless sports of middle life; it is our greatest pride that they do – albeit tearfully – send us fearless and erect, to lead the backward races into line. 'Surely we are the people!' Shall it be the Little Englander for whom the Norman fought the Saxon on his field? Was it for him the archers bled at

Crecy and Poitiers, or Cromwell drilled his men? Is it only
for the desk our youngsters read of Drake and Frobisher, of
Nelson, Clive and men like Mungo Park? Is it for the count-
ing-house they learn of Carthage, Greece and Rome? No, no;
a thousand times no! The British race will take its place, the
British blood will tell. Son after son will leave the Mersey,
strong in the will of his parents today, stronger in the deed
of his fathers in the past, braving the climate, taking the risks,
playing his best in the game of life.' (pp. 39–40.)

Moreover, and as in *Things Fall Apart*, the fact of trade, the
liberating effect of money gained through competitive trade and
the political possibilities which freedom and wealth offer are
seen as accounting for the rapid changes which disrupt traditional
life and values. Consider the following speech by John Nwodika,
kinsman of Ezeulu and servant in Winterbottom's household.
Here too the continuity of theme with *Things Fall Apart* is suggested
in references to Umuofia, Mbaino, and so on:

'I know that some people at home have been spreading the
story that I cook for the white man. Your brother does not
see even the smoke from his fire; I just put things in order in
his house. You know the white man is not like us; if he puts
this plate here he will be angry if you have it there. So I go
round every day and see that everything is in its right place.
But I can tell you that I do not aim to die a servant. My eye is
on starting a small trade in tobacco as soon as I have collected
a little money. People from other places are gathering much
wealth in this trade and in the trade for cloth. People from
Elumelu, Aninta, Umuofia, Mbaino, they control the great
new market. They decide what goes on in it. Is there one
Umuaro man among the wealthy people here? Not one. Sometimes I feel shame when others ask me where I come from.
We have no share in the market; we have no share in the
white man's office; we have no share anywhere. That was
why I rejoiced when the white man called me the other day
and told me that there was a wise man in my village and that
his name was Ezeulu. I told him yes. He asked if he was still
alive and I said yes. He said: 'Go with the Head Messenger
and tell him that I have a few questions I want to ask him

about the custom of his people because I know he is a wise
man.' I said to myself: 'This is our chance to bring our clan
in front of the white men.' (p. 210.)

And, further, he records the advice given him by a clansman about
the importance of money:

> 'He said the race for the white man's money would not
> wait till tomorrow or till we were ready to join; if the rat
> could not run fast enough it must make way for the tortoise.
> He said other people from every small clan – some people
> we used to despise – they were all now in high favour when
> our own people did not even know that day had broken.'
> (p. 209.)

Ezeulu is allowed to remain in the guardhouse for several days
and he is content enough since he is intent on learning the white
man's motive in bringing him to Okperi. At last Clarke, who has
taken over from Winterbottom during the latter's illness, tells
him of the Government's plan for him:

> After that he calmed down and spoke about the benefits of
> the British Administration. Clarke had not wanted to deliver
> this lecture which he would have called complacent if some-
> body else had spoken it. But he could not help himself. Con-
> fronted with the proud inattention of this fetish priest whom
> they were about to do a great favour by elevating him above
> his fellows and who, instead of gratitude, returned scorn,
> Clarke did not know what else to say. The more he spoke the
> more he became angry.
> In the end thanks to his considerable self-discipline and
> the breathing space afforded by the off-and-on of talking
> through an interpreter Clarke was able to rally and rescue
> himself. Then he made the proposal to Ezeulu.
> The expression on the priest's face did not change when
> the news was broken to him. He remained silent. Clarke knew
> it would take a little time for the proposal to strike him with
> its full weight.
> 'Well, are you accepting the offer or not?' Clarke glowed
> with the I-know-this-will-knock-you-over-feeling of a bene-
> factor.

'Tell the white man that Ezeulu will not be anybody's chief,
except Ulu.'

'What!' shouted Clarke. 'Is the fellow mad?'

'I tink so sah,' said the interpreter.

'In that case he goes back to prison.' Clarke was now really
angry. What cheek! A witch-doctor making a fool of the
British Administration in public! (p. 215.)

This scene presents the crisis in the novel and from it all subsequent action flows and its resolution is achieved. It is also the
culminating point in a theme which Achebe has been exploring
since the beginning of the book – the analysis or evaluation of the
practicality of the system of indirect rule which forms the basis of
British administration in Nigeria and which is described as follows
in a memorandum received by Winterbottom and sent by the
Lieutenant-Governor:

'My purpose in these paragraphs is limited to impressing on
all Political Officers working among tribes who lack Natural
Rulers the vital necessity of developing without any further
delay an effective system of "indirect rule" based on native
institutions.'

'To many colonial nations native administration means
government by white men. You are all aware that H.M.G. con-
siders this policy as mistaken. In place of the alternative of
governing directly through Administrative Officers there is
the other method of trying while we endeavour to purge the
native system of its abuses to build a higher civilization upon
the soundly rooted native stock that had its foundation in the
hearts and minds and thoughts of the people and therefore on
which we can more easily build, moulding it and establishing
it into lines consonant with modern ideas and higher standards, and yet all the time enlisting the real force of the
spirit of the people, instead of killing all that out and trying
to start afresh. We must not destroy the African atmosphere,
the African mind, the whole foundation of his race. . . .'
(pp. 67–8.)

The directive states the ideal of indirect rule. Winterbottom's reaction:

'Words, words, words. Civilization. African mind, African
atmosphere. Has His Honour ever rescued a man buried
alive up to his neck, with a piece of roast yam on his head to
attract vultures?' He began to pace up and down again. But
why couldn't someone tell the bloody man that the whole
damn thing was stupid and futile. He knew why. They were all
afraid of losing their promotion or the O.B.E. (p. 68)

suggests the difficulty in realizing the ideal. Winterbottom further
muses on the fact that, as he sees it, 'the great tragedy of British
colonial administration was that the man on the spot who knew his
African and knew what he was talking about found himself being
constantly overruled by starry-eyed fellows at headquarters.' (p. 68.)
Winterbottom is a 'pagan man', a man who thinks he knows his
tribe better than those who control and administer policy from
government headquarters but with little experience on the ground.
Winterbottom is correct in his assessment to the extent that he
recognizes the harm done by the creation of warrant chief and
systems of kingship 'among a people who never had kings before!
This is what British Administration was doing among the Ibos,
making a dozen mushroom kings grow where none grew before.'
(p. 70.) The case of James Ikedi, a mission-educated man who was
created a warrant chief and used his office to establish a complicated system of bribery and corruption is cited by Winterbottom
as the most dangerous consequence of the system of indirect rule.
Not only does the career of Ikenga, a Christian, standing as it does
in direct contrast with Ezeulu's refusal to accept the offer of
warrant chief, indicate the debasing effect of colonial practices in
Ibo life, a fact which Winterbottom understands, but it indicates
as well that despite his alleged understanding Winterbottom is as
incompetent as his seniors. It is ironic that he has chosen Ezeulu
because of the latter's seeming support of British administration
over the Okperi land issue without taking the trouble to find out
what Ezeulu's real motives were: that is, he stood on the side of
right, as he saw it, within his community and it is purely accidental
that this judgement was coincidental as Winterbottom's determina-
tion.

Achebe displays considerable skill and gains considerable effect
from his careful handling of the scenes devoted to Winterbottom.

Not many pages of the novel are given over to him; nor are his opinions explored at any great depth, when compared to those of Ezeulu musing on his circumstances. And this is an exact reflection of the historical and cultural reality the book creates. Chapter Two of the novel which runs to eighteen pages is given over almost entirely to the causes of the war with Okperi over the piece of land. Achebe relates this to the intricate structure of kinship which exists between the villages, to questions of religion and other responsibilities and includes a consideration of the personal motives which dictate the actions of the supporters of Nwaka on the one hand and Ezeulu on the other. In Chapter Three we are introduced to Winterbottom and given, in a page, his assured summing up of the cause of the war in which he intervened. Achebe's treatment is ironic and his intention is to suggest and confirm at the outset the very real lack of apprehension among Europeans of Ibo customs and to counterpoint this with the assurance, not to say arrogance, with which they involve themselves and control Ibo life. Winterbottom is speaking:

'This war between Umuaro and Okperi began in a rather interesting way. I went into it in considerable detail. . . . this war started because a man from Umuaro went to visit a friend in Okperi one fine morning and after he'd had one or two gallons of palm-wine – it's quite incredible how much of that dreadful stuff they can tuck away – anyhow, this man from Umuaro having drunk his friend's palm-wine reached for his *ikenga* and split it in two. I may explain that *ikenga* is the most important fetish in the Ibo man's arsenal, so to speak. It represents his ancestors to whom he must make daily sacrifice. When he dies it is split in two, one half is buried with him and the other half is thrown away. So you can see the implication of what our friend from Umuaro did in splitting his host's fetish. This was, of course, the greatest sacrilege. The outraged host reached for his gun and blew the other fellow's head off. And so a regular war developed between the two villages, until I stepped in. I went into the question of the ownership of the piece of land which was the remote cause of all the unrest and found without any shade of doubt that it belonged to Okperi. I should mention that every witness who testified before me – from both sides without exception – perjured themselves. One thing you must remember in dealing with natives is that like children they are great liars. They don't lie simply to get out of trouble. Sometimes they would spoil a good case by a pointless lie. Only one man – a kind of priest-king in Umuaro – witnessed against his own people. I have not found out what it was, but I think he must have had some pretty fierce tabu working on him. But he was a most impressive figure of a man. He was very light in complexion, almost red. One finds people like that now and again among the Ibos. I have a theory that the Ibos in the distant past assimilated a small non-negroid tribe of the same complexion as the Red Indians.' (pp. 45–6.)

The passage reveals that Winterbottom's failure to get the facts of the land dispute – the 'remote' cause of the unrest – proceeds from his arrogance and this in turn causes him to consider Ezeulu acceptable because the priest did not 'perjure' himself. That he failed utterly to understand Ezeulu and the traditions and conventions which he represents is signified by Ezeulu's refusal to accept the offer of a warrant chieftaincy. Ezeulu is insulted by the patronage the offer implies, and realizes now that the white man is a communal enemy and must be made to pay for the insult offered.

Nevertheless his concern is not so much with the white man, his dominant feeling is that 'he had settled his little score with the white man and could forget him for the moment', but his 'struggle was with his own people and the white man was, without knowing it, his ally.' (p. 217.) There is a complicated kind of irony and paradox at work here. Before going to Government Hill Ezeulu was seen by his enemies at home as being in league with the white man. His enemies had made much of this. His rejection of the offer made by Clarke is at first greeted with suspicion by them:

At first few people in Umuaro believed the story that Ezeulu had rejected the white man's offer to be a Warrant Chief. How could he refuse the very thing he had been planning and scheming for all these years? his enemies asked. (p. 217.)

The fact that he remains in jail for so long a time convinces them

of his sincerity and his reputation rises. Now Ezeulu determines to
have his revenge on his people for the distrust of him and their
failure to heed his counsel:

> His quarrel with the white man was insignificant beside
> the matter he must settle with his own people. For years he
> had been warning Umuaro not to allow a few jealous men to
> lead them into the bush. But they had stopped both ears with
> fingers. They had gone on taking one dangerous step after
> another and now they had gone too far. They had taken
> away too much for the owner not to notice. Now the fight
> must take place, for until a man wrestles with one of those
> who make a path across his homestead the others will not stop.
> Ezeulu's muscles tingled for the fight. Let the white man
> detain him not for one day but one year so that his deity not
> seeing him in his place would ask Umuaro questions. (p. 198.)

While he remains in prison Ezeulu has a prophetic dream which
foreshadows his final position although at the time Ezeulu sees
it merely as an analogy of the disregard in which he is held by his
people:

> That night Ezeulu saw in a dream a big assembly of Umuaro
> elders, the same people he had spoken to a few days earlier.
> But instead of himself it was his grandfather who rose up to
> speak to them. They refused to listen. They shouted together:
> 'He will not speak; we shall not listen to him.' The Chief Priest
> raised his voice and pleaded with them to listen but they re-
> fused saying that they must bale the water while it was still
> only ankle-deep. 'Why should we rely on him to tell us the
> season of the year?' asked Nwaka. 'Is there anybody here who
> cannot see the moon in his own compound? And anyhow what
> is the power of Ulu today? He saved our fathers from the
> warriors of Abam but he cannot save us from the white man.
> Let us drive him away as our neighbours of Aninta drove out
> and burnt Ogba when he left what he was called to do and
> did other things, when he turned round to kill the people of
> Aninta instead of their enemies.' Then the people seized the
> Chief Priest who had changed from Ezeulu's grandfather to
> himself and began to push him from one group to another.

Some spat on his face and called him the priest of a dead god. (pp. 196–7.)

Ironically at the time that these thoughts pass through Ezeulu's mind their full implication lost on him, his son, Nwafo, the heir-apparent to the office of Ezeulu, almost saves his father from the calamity which ultimately overtakes him. Nwafo muses:

As night drew near Nwafo's mind returned to the thought which had been troubling him since yesterday. What would happen to the new moon? He knew his father had been expecting it before he went away. Would it follow him to Okperi or would it wait for his return? If it appeared in Okperi with what metal gong would Ezeulu receive it? Nwafo looked at the *ogene* which lay by the wall, the stick with which it was beaten showing at its mouth. The best solution was for the new moon to wait for his return tomorrow.

However as dusk came down Nwafo took his position where his father always sat. He did not wait very long before he saw the young thin moon. It looked very thin and reluctant. Nwafo reached for the *ogene* and made to beat it but fear stopped his hand. (p. 205.)

Ezeulu delights in contemplating his revenge. Achebe uses an appropriate image to suggest the quality of Ezeulu's thoughts: 'Ezeulu was like a puff-adder which never struck until it had unlocked its seven deadly fangs one after the other. If while it did this its tormentor did not have the good sense to run for its life it would only have itself to blame.' (p. 220.) And again: 'That was the terror of the puff-adder: it would suffer every provocation, it would even let the enemy step on its trunk; it must wait and unlock its seven deadly fangs one after the other. Then it would be death to its tormentor.'

Upon his return home, however, he receives a hero's welcome and his anger is assuaged:

As long as he was in exile it was easy for Ezeulu to think of Umuaro as one hostile entity. But back in his hut he could no longer see the matter as simply as that. . . . Ezeulu continued his division of Umuaro into ordinary people who had nothing but goodwill for him and those others whose ambition sought to destroy the central unity of the six villages. From the moment he made this division thoughts of reconciliation began, albeit timidly, to visit him. He knew he could say with justice that if one finger brought oil it messed up the others; but was it right that he should stretch his hand against all these people who had shown so much concern for him during his exile and since his return? (pp. 230–1.)

But thoughts of reconciliation are blunted by his God who visits him:

Meanwhile Ezeulu had pursued again his thoughts on the coming struggle and begun to probe with the sensitiveness of a snail's horns the possibility of reconciliation or, if that was too much, of narrowing down the area of conflict. Behind his thinking was of course the knowledge that the fight would not begin until the time of harvest, after three moons more. So there was plenty of time. Perhaps it was this knowledge that there was no hurry which gave him confidence to play with alternatives – to dissolve his resolution and at the right time form it again. Why should a man be in a hurry to lick his fingers; was he going to put them away in the rafter? Or perhaps the thoughts of reconciliation were from a true source. But whatever it was, Ezeulu was not to be allowed to remain in two minds much longer.

'Ta! Nwanu!' barked Ulu in his ear, as a spirit would in the ear of an impertinent human child. 'Who told you that this was your own fight?'

Ezeulu trembled and said nothing.

'I say who told you that this was your own fight which you could arrange to suit you? You want to save your friends who brought you palm-wine he-he-he-he-he!' laughed the deity the way spirits do – a dry skeletal laugh. 'Beware you do not come between me and my victim or you may receive blows not meant for you! Do you not know what happens when two elephants fight? Go home and sleep and leave me to settle my quarrel with Idemili, who wants to destroy me so that his python may come to power. Now you tell me how it concerns you. I say go home and sleep. As for me and Idemili we shall fight to the finish; and whoever throws the other down will strip him of his anklet!'

D

After that there was no more to be said. Who was Ezeulu
to tell his deity how to fight the jealous cult of the sacred
python? It was a fight of the gods. He was no more than an
arrow in the bow of his god. (pp. 240–1.)

The irony here is an important and complex one. Ezeulu determines in the first instance to revenge himself on the villagers
partly from personal motives because his advice to them has been
ignored, but mostly because he fears that the unity of the village
will be destroyed. He then shifts his position and fears that through
taking revenge the things he seeks to avoid, the breaking up of the
cohesion of the village, will take place. In the end it is taken from
his hands and what he fears, takes place.

At the injunction of his god he exacts his revenge on his people.
The Feast of the New Yam is approaching and it is at this time,
when the village is most vulnerable, that Ezeulu intends to hit
Umuaro. In one of the few purely explanatory passages in the
novel Achebe writes:

This feast was the end of the old year and the beginning of
the new. Before it a man might dig up a few yams around his
house to ward off hunger in his family but no one would
begin the harvesting of the big farms. And, in any case, no man
of title would taste new yam from whatever source before the
festival. It reminded the six villages of their coming together
in ancient times and of their continuing debt to Ulu who saved
them from the ravages of the Abam. At every New Yam feast
the coming together of the villages was re-enacted and every
grown man in Umuaro took a good-sized seed-yam to the
shrine of Ulu and placed it in the heap from his village after
circling it round his head; then he took the lump of chalk
lying beside the heap and marked his face. It was from these
heaps that the elders knew the number of men in each village.
If there was an increase over the previous year a sacrifice of
gratitude was made to Ulu; but if the number had declined the
reason was sought from diviners and a sacrifice of appeasement
was ordered. It was also from these yams that Ezeulu selected
thirteen with which to reckon the new year.

If the festival meant no more than this it would still be the
most important ceremony in Umuaro. But it was also the day

for all the minor deities in the six villages who did not have their own special feasts. On that day each of these gods was brought by its custodian and stood in a line outside the shrine of Ulu so that any man or woman who had received a favour from it could make a small present in return. This was the one public appearance these smaller gods were allowed in the year. They rode into the market place on the heads or shoulders of their custodians, danced round and then stood side by side at the entrance to the shrine of Ulu. Some of them would be very old nearing the time when their power would be transferred to new carvings and they would be cast aside; and some would have been made only the other day. The very old ones carried face marks like the man who made them, in the days before Umuaro abandoned the custom. At last year's festival only three of these ancients were left. Perhaps this year one or two more would disappear, following the men who made them in their own image and departed long ago.

The festival thus brought gods and men together in one crowd. It was the only assembly in Umuaro in which a man might look to his right and find his neighbour and look to his left and see a god standing there – perhaps Agwu whose mother also gave birth to madness or Ngene, owner of a stream. (pp. 253–4.)

Ezeulu's customary function is to announce the beginning of each new month and to eat one of the ceremonial yams which signifies its passing. While he was in jail two new moons occurred thus two months were not declared nor the yams assigned to them eaten – that is the time they represented had not passed. Ezeulu refuses to announce the Feast of the New Yam, two months pass, the ground hardens and the new harvest is lost. Ezeulu, his family and the villagers suffer. Ezeulu does not act out of personal spite nor the desire to redress insult to himself. Were this so his actions and his fate in the closing chapter of the novel would lack convincingness and point.

. . . the heaviest load was on Ezeulu's mind. He was used to loneliness. As Chief Priest he had always walked alone in front of Umuaro. But without looking back he had always been able to hear their flute and song which shook the earth because it

came from a multitude of voices and the stamping of countless
feet. There had been moments when the voices were divided
as in the matter of the land dispute with Okperi. But never
until now had he known the voices to die away altogether. Few
people came to his hut now and those who came said nothing.
Ezeulu wanted to hear what Umuaro was saying but nobody
volunteered the information and he would not make anyone
think he was curious. So with every passing day Umuaro became more and more an alien silence – the kind of silence
which burnt a man's inside like the blue, quiet, razor-edge
flame of burning palm-nut shells. Ezeulu writhed in the pain
which grew and grew until he wanted to get outside his compound or even into the Nkwo market place and shout at
Umuaro.

Because no one came near enough to Ezeulu to see his
anguish – and if they had seen it they would not have understood – they imagined that he sat in his hut gloating over the
distress of Umuaro. But although he would not for any reason
see the present trend reversed he carried more punishment
and more suffering than all his fellows. What troubled him
most – and he alone seemed to be aware of it at present – was
that the punishment was not for now alone but for all time.
It would afflict Umuaro like an *ogulu-aro* disease which counts
a year and returns to its victim. Beneath all anger in his mind
lay a deeper compassion for Umuaro, the clan which long,
long ago when lizards were in ones and twos chose his ancestor
to carry their deity and go before them challenging every
obstacle and confronting every danger on their behalf. (pp.
273–4.)

And this evaluation is confirmed by Akuebue, 'the only man
in Umuaro who knew that Ezeulu was not deliberately punishing
the six villages as some people thought. He knew that the Chief
Priest was helpless: that a greater thing than *nté* was caught in
nté's trap.' (p. 275.) He sees, as does Ezeulu, that the priest is no
more than an 'arrow in the bow of his god'. Achebe has prepared
the way for Ezeulu's final actions early in the book when he has
him muse on the nature of his power:

Whenever Ezeulu considered the immensity of his power

over the year and the crops and, therefore, over the people he wondered if it was real. It was true he named the day for the feast of the Pumpkin Leaves and for the New Yam feast; but he did not choose the day. He was merely a watchman. His power was no more than the power of a child over a goat that was said to be his. As long as the goat was alive it was his; he would find it food and take care of it. But the day it was slaughtered he would know who the real owner was. No! the Chief Priest of Ulu was more than that, must be more than that. If he should refuse to name the day there would be no festival – no planting and no reaping. But could he refuse? No Chief Priest had ever refused. So it could not be done. He would not dare. (pp. 3–4.)

Similar passages throughout the book reveal the effort Ezeulu makes to understand his power while at the same time revealing that he never deviates from the service of his god. He accepts as unquestionable the directives of Ulu. In the end he is defeated by the god himself, for Ulu, the creation of the people at a time of intense need, is rejected by the people in like circumstances when he is seen to conspire against them. Ogbuefi Ofaka's speculation that 'perhaps a god like Ulu leads a priest to ruin himself' (p. 216) proves accurate, and Akuebue's words 'a saying of our ancestors, that when brothers fight to death a stranger inherits their father's estate' (p. 275) proves prophetic.

The climax of the novel is reached with the death of Obika, the proudest of Ezeulu's sons. Asked by grieving villagers to perform as Ogbazulobodo, the night spirit who chases away evil spirits, Obika agrees, though ill with a dangerous fever. His reason is simple: 'If I say no they will say that Ezeulu and his family have sworn to wreck the second burial of their village man who did no harm.' Obika, dressed in the regalia of Ogbazulobodo makes his run through the villages:

A fire began to rage inside his chest and to push a dry bitterness up his mouth. But he tasted it from a distance or from a mouth within his mouth. He felt like two separate persons, one running above the other.

'. . . When a handshake passes the elbow it becomes another thing. The sleep that lasts from one market day to another has become death. The man who likes the meat of the funeral ram, why does he recover when sickness visits him? The mighty tree falls and the little birds scatter in the bush. . . . The little bird which hops off the ground and lands on an ant-hill may not know it but is still on the ground. . . . A common snake which a man sees all alone may become a python in his eyes. . . . The very Thing which kills Mother Rat is always there to make sure that its young ones never open their eyes. . . . The boy who persists in asking what happened to his father before he has enough strength to avenge him is asking for his father's fate. . . . The man who belittles the sickness which Monkey has suffered should ask to see the eyes which his nurse got from blowing the sick fire. . . . When death wants to take a little dog it prevents it from smelling even excrement. . . .' (p. 282–3.)

The exertion is too much for the sick Obika and death is the result. Achebe writes:

Ezeulu sank to the ground in utter amazement. It was not simply the blow of Obika's death, great though it was. Men had taken greater blows; that was what made a man a man. They say a man is like a funeral ram which must take whatever beating comes to it without opening its mouth; only the silent tremor of pain down its body tells of its suffering.

At any other time Ezeulu would have been more than equal to any grief not compounded with humiliation. Why, he asked himself again and again, why had Ulu chosen to deal thus with him, to strike him down and cover him with mud? What was his offence? Had he not divined the god's will and obeyed it? When was it ever heard that a child was scalded by the piece of yam its own mother put in its palm? What man would send his son with a potsherd to bring fire from a neighbour's hut and then unleash rain on him? Who ever sent his son up the palm to gather nuts and then took an axe and felled the tree? But today such a thing had happened before the eyes of all. What could it point to but the collapse and ruin of all things? Then a god, finding himself powerless might take to his heels and in one final, backward glance at his abandoned worshippers cry:

> If the rat cannot flee fast enough
> Let him make way for the tortoise!

Perhaps it was the constant, futile throbbing of these thoughts that finally left a crack in Ezeulu's mind. Or perhaps his implacable assailant having stood over him for a little while stepped on him as on an insect and crushed him in the dust. But this final act of malevolence proved merciful. It allowed Ezeulu, in his last days, to live in the haughty splendour of a demented high priest and spared him knowledge of the final outcome. (pp. 286–7.)

Irony of a kind similar to that of the close of *Things Fall Apart* informs the conclusion of the novel:

> So in the end only Umuaro and its leaders saw the final outcome. To them the issue was simple. Their god had taken sides with them against his headstrong and ambitious priest and thus upheld the wisdom of their ancestors – that no man however great was greater than his people; that no man ever won judgement against his clan.
>
> If this was so then Ulu had chosen a dangerous time to uphold this wisdom. In destroying his priest he had also brought disaster on himself, like the lizard in the fable who ruined his mother's funeral by his own hand. For a deity who chose a time such as this to destroy his priest or abandon him to his enemies was inciting people to take liberties; and Umuaro was just ripe to do so. The Christian harvest which took place a few days after Obika's death saw more people than even Goodcountry could have dreamed. In his extremity many an Umuaro man had sent his son with a yam or two to offer to the new religion and to bring back the promised immunity. Thereafter any yam that was harvested in the man's fields was harvested in the name of the son. (p. 287.)

And Akuebue's fear that 'no man however great can win judgement against the clan' and his recognition that 'when brothers fight a stranger inherits their father's estate' are proven.

Achebe's theme here, as in *Things Fall Apart*, is the inexorable flow of history consolidated in the tragic fate of a hero who epitomizes his times. The triumph of Christianity is brought about, ironically, by its principal antagonist. Ezeulu possesses the characteristics of the classical tragic hero – a man of power and influence in his community, a leader who epitomizes the spirit of his times. A man, too, with a tragic flaw, arrogance and pride, which causes him to commit an error in judgement when he lets his personal feelings interfere with his usually keen assessment of circumstances. Even so, he acts on the injunction of his God and the seeming ambiguity this implies accounts for the series of ironic reversals he experiences – the loss of the loyalty of Udoche, the death of Obika who dies to preserve his father's reputation, and the compounded irony in the fact that Obika's death precipitates Ezeulu's collapse. Finally, there is the overwhelming irony implicit in the triumph of Christianity, as it were by accident. The white man has been a passive agent in seeing his way triumph. As Achebe says: 'It looked as though the gods and the power of events finding Winterbottom handy used him and left him again in order as they found him.' The sense of tragic pity the novel evokes results from the fact that Ezeulu's actions have been well-intentioned and meant to serve the general good. History, unconcerned, passes him by and he is allowed to live out his life 'in the haughty splendour of a demented high priest'.

In this book perhaps better than in any of the novels, Achebe realizes his artistic intention to the full. His joint purpose in his writing is, as we have seen, both instructive and imaginative. *Arrow of God* at one level shows us a section of Ibo society in the first decade of the twentieth century under the pressure of colonial rule. It presents, that is, a particular and important point of transition and characters who convince us that they are true representatives of that society, a society with a tightly organized system of beliefs – social, political and religious – understood by all members of the society and by which they conduct their lives. It is a society possessed of humane needs and values, and dignity, and these qualities are made clear by the casual way in which they are affronted by the representatives of the colonial power and by the display of the contradictoriness and ambiguousness of the ways in which that power operates. In this sense *Arrow of God* displays Achebe's utilitarian purposes and everything in it is relative, particular and historical.

Yet Achebe's overall intention is to explore the depths of the human condition and in this other and more important sense *Arrow of God* transcends its setting and shows us characters whose values, motivations, actions and qualities are permanent in human kind.

It is Achebe's achievement in the first three novels to see and present life over a long stretch of time, to present characters who appear and disappear in a cycle of recurring movement without taking anything away from the urgency of the present. The past, presented in both personal and societal terms is brought before us vividly and tragically for a time and then made to recede. The closing pages of each of the three novels reveal Achebe's intention of putting us at a distance from the actions which a moment before have been intense and immediate. The effect is to realize intensely the personal and societal tragedies and then to place them in the inevitable ebb and flow of human history.

Achebe's plots follow a strict and logical development. His method is essentially dramatic. Nothing is out of place. Yet there is a paradox apparent in the overall effect the novels create. As has been seen Achebe's view is essentially tragic and a sense of immediacy and finality is communicated when the tragedy has finally taken place. The effect of the final passages of the novels in placing these events into their historical context is to give a different value to the particular events in the novel – to make the tragic pathetic, the inevitable accidental, the final relative and to communicate the sense that this is natural and inevitable.

There are few compromises with or concessions to the reader in *Arrow of God* which, because of the complexities of the finely wrought plot supported by an intricately patterned series of ambiguities and ironies, set against a background equally intricately patterned and the whole couched in a language everywhere appropriate to the themes, only yields its full meaning through careful and deliberate readings.

A Man of the People

▼▼▼▼▼▼▼▼▼▼▼▼▼▼▼▼▼▼▼▼▼▼▼▼▼▼▼▼▼▼▼▼

A MAN OF THE PEOPLE marks a change in Achebe's approach to novel writing. In the first three books he explored in various ways the results of the confrontation between Africa and Europe and centred his novels in the stories of heroes whose lives end tragically, partly because of flaws in their natures which cause them to make miscalculations at critical moments, and partly because they are caught up in historical circumstances which they are powerless to control and which overcome them. Achebe's approach in these books is insistently ironic but it is the irony which attaches to tragedy. In *A Man of the People* which is set in post-independence Nigeria and treats events almost exactly contemporary with its writing, Achebe employs the irony of the satirist in order to ridicule and condemn the circumstances the book evokes and which determine its moral pattern. In this regard Achebe says of the book:

> *A Man of the People* is a rather serious indictment – if you like – on post-independence Africa. But I don't despair because I think this is a necessary stage in our growth. . . . If you take the example of Nigeria, which is the place I know best, things had got to such a point politically that there was no other answer – no way you could resolve this impasse politically. The political machine had been so abused that whichever way you pressed it, it produced the same results; and therefore another force had to come in. Now when I was writing *A Man of the People* it wasn't clear to me that this was going to be necessarily military intervention. It could easily have been civil war, which in fact it very nearly was in Nigeria. But I think the next generation of politicians in Nigeria, when we do have them, will have learned one or two

lessons, I hope, from what happened to the First Republic. This is the only hope I have and if it turns out to be vain, it would be terrible. . . .[23]

This then is the situation the book describes and it did offer at the time of its publication, as many have observed, an uncanny prediction on the course events were to follow.

Certain of the themes which were prominent in the earlier books are here completely re-interpreted, most noticeably what we have called the 'colonial theme'. Europe has no direct influence, of the kind described in *Things Fall Apart*, *No Longer at Ease* or *Arrow of God*, in the affairs of the post-independent state, although there are indications that Europeans are deeply enmeshed in the complicated system of bribery and corruption which informs the political life of the community. However, the legacy of colonialism is apparent. The breakdown in the continuity and unity of tribal life vested in the intricate balance between the pursuit of material things and the observance of religious customs and traditions which had its beginnings in the situation described in *Things Fall Apart* and further elaborated in *Arrow of God* and *No Longer at Ease* is complete in *A Man of the People*. In the first three books, religious observances though hard-pressed to survive in an increasingly acquisitive world, were still capable of influencing the actions and consciences of men. The emasculation of traditional religion is complete by the time of the action of *A Man of the People*. Achebe conveys this powerfully in a very brief scene. The brevity of the scene and the nature of the religious comment made offers an exact ironic reflection of the efficacy of the restraining force of the traditional religion in the contemporary social situation. It is Christmas time and the hero of the novel, Odili, is visiting the wife of Chief Nanga, M.P. Among other things, comment is made on the new house which is being built for Nanga. One townsman says:

'Look at the new house he is building. Four storeys! Before, if a man built two storeys the whole town would come to admire it. But today my kinsman is building four.'*

---

*Achebe, Chinua, *A Man of the People*. Heinemann Educational Books 1966, p. 108. All page references in this chapter are to this edition, though page numbers are identical in the cased edition by William Heinemann 1966.

And Odili, who is telling the story, observes:

> The house in question was the very modern four-storey
> structure going up beside the present building and which was
> to get into the news later. It was, as we were to learn, a 'dash'
> from the European building firm of Antonio and Sons whom
> Nanga had recently given the half-million pound contract to
> build the National Academy of Arts and Sciences (p. 108)

thus specifying the total corruption of perhaps the most responsible
and influential Minister next to the Prime Minister. At the same
time as comment is made on the house, a group of masked boy
dancers entertain the Christmas guests. Achebe writes:

> The last, its wooden mask-face a little askew and its stuffed
> pot-belly looking really stuffed, was held in restraint by his
> attendants tugging at a rope tied round his waist as adult
> attendants do to a real, dangerous Mask. The children sang,
> beat drums, gongs and cigarette cups and the Mask danced
> comically to the song:

> > Sunday, bigi bele Sunday
> > Sunday, bigi bele Sunday
> > Akatakata done come!
> > Everybody run away!
> > Sunday, Alleluia!

> While the Mask danced here and there brandishing an
> outsize matchet the restraining rope round his waist came
> undone. One might have expected this sudden access to
> freedom to be followed by a wild rampage and loss of life and
> property. But the Mask tamely put his matchet down, helped
> his disciples retie the rope, picked up his weapon again and
> resumed his dance. (pp. 108–9.)

The Masks, the symbols of the religious element in the community who heretofore represented the continuity of religious
experience within the tribe, are reduced to the status of enter-
tainers.[24] All but the most superficial accretion of religion has
vanished. Achebe has written elsewhere a comment which
illuminates the intention and importance of the dramatic scene
recorded above:

A man's position in society was usually determined by his wealth. All the four titles in my village were taken – not given – and each had its own price. But in those days wealth meant the strength of your arm. No one became rich by swindling the community or stealing government money. In fact a man who was guilty of theft immediately lost all his titles. Today we have kept the materialism and thrown away the spirituality which should keep it in check.[25]

The novel, then, is a comment on the degree to which acquisitiveness and unrestrained corruption have come to dominate Nigerian life. The novel tells, in the first person, the story of Odili Kamalu, a university graduate and secondary school teacher, and of his involvement with Chief the Honourable M. N. Nanga, M.P., and with the political life of the country. In many ways Odili resembles Obi Okonkwo of *No Longer at Ease*. He is young, a university graduate, and therefore part of the new élite of the country. He possesses idealism and a desire to create a better country than that in which he lives. Like that of Obi Okonkwo, Odili's idealism is directed towards promotion of the general good in the country. The moral centre of the book is found here. But unlike Obi's idealism, Odili's is tempered by an awareness of practical realities and a capacity for decisive if not always serviceable action. Obi fails through a too careful consideration of the opposing forces which hedge him round. Odili cuts through qualifications and rationalizations and acts in support of his beliefs. Odili is the man Obi might have become.

The novel falls more or less evenly into two parts. At first scornful of Nanga's fraudulent political behaviour and understanding the devious and dishonest means by which Nanga has achieved prominence, Odili is nevertheless nearly overwhelmed by Nanga's charisma and seduced to his opportunistic way of thinking and acting. He accepts an invitation to be Nanga's guest in the capital city and there sees at first hand the extravagant life lived by senior members of government, an extravagance supported largely through defrauding the people by a very thinly disguised system of bribery, corruption and nepotism. Of his experiences gained through this brief but intense association with Nanga Odili writes:

My host was one of those people around whom things were always happening. I must always remain grateful to him for the insight I got into the affairs of our country during my brief stay in his house. From the day a few years before when I had left Parliament depressed and aggrieved, I had felt, like so many other educated citizens of our country, that things were going seriously wrong without being able to say just how. We complained about our country's lack of dynamism and abdication of the leadership to which it was entitled in the continent, or so we thought. We listened to whispers of scandalous deals in high places – sometimes involving sums of money that I for one didn't believe existed in the country. But there was really no hard kernel of fact to get one's teeth into. But sitting at Chief Nanga's feet I received enlightenment; many things began to crystallize out of the mist – some of the emergent forms were not nearly us ugly as I had suspected but many seemed much worse. However, I was not making these judgements at the time, or not strongly anyhow. I was simply too fascinated by the almost ritual lifting of the clouds, as I had been one day, watching for the first time the unveiling of the white dome of Kilimanjaro at sunset. (pp. 44–5.)

When Nanga steals his mistress from him, Odili, initially from motives of revenge, but principally because of a political idealism which re-asserts itself, joins a new and rival political party founded by a barrister friend. This marks the beginning of the second part of the novel. The new party is founded because the leader, Maxwell Kulamo and 'some of his friends, [who] having watched with deepening disillusion the use to which our hard-won independence was being put by corrupt, mediocre politicians had decided to come together and launch the Common People's Convention.' (p. 87.) A sudden, though not entirely unexpected financial crisis threatens to undermine the government and an election is called. Odili is chosen to contest the seat held by Nanga. He pursues the election with little hope of winning yet with complete integrity. If he is not entirely certain what the defeat of Nanga and his corrupt colleagues will produce, he is confirmed in his belief that they must go. Yet such is his cynicism that he cannot wholly

believe Nanga will be repudiated by the electorate. 'How important,' Odili muses,

> . . . was my political activity in its own right? It was difficult
> to say; things seemed so mixed up; my revenge, my new politi-
> cal ambition and the girl. And perhaps it was just as well that
> my motives should entangle and reinforce one another. For I
> was not being so naïve as to imagine that loving Edna was
> enough to wrench her from a minister. True, I had other
> advantages like youth and education but those were nothing
> beside wealth and position and the authority of a greedy
> father. No. I needed all the reinforcement I could get.
> Although I had little hope of winning Chief Nanga's seat, it
> was necessary nonetheless to fight and expose him as much as
> possible so that, even if he won, the Prime Minister would find
> it impossible to re-appoint him to his Cabinet. In fact there
> was already enough filth clinging to his name to disqualify
> him – and most of his colleagues as well – but we are not as
> strict as some countries. That is why C.P.C. publicity had to
> ferret out every scandal and blow it up, and maybe someone
> would get up and say: 'No, Nanga has taken more than the
> owner could ignore!' But it was no more than a hope (pp.
> 121–2.)

Odili's forecast is correct. He has little chance of beating Nanga
even though the latter fears what Odili represents – the young,
educated Nigerian whose actions are disinterested in the political
sense that he and his peers seek to restitute a constitution whose
prerogatives and guarantees have become vestigial. Odili is entirely scrupulous in this respect and is grieved when Max accepts
a large bribe from Chief Koko to withdraw from the election. Max
uses the money to support his own campaign.

Nanga and his colleagues bring considerable resources to bear in
running their campaign – control of the national broadcasting
system and newspapers, bands of hired thugs masquerading as
policemen, and financial support from sources outside the country
but with huge vested interests in it.

> Do you know, Odili, that British Amalgamated has paid
> out four hundred thousand pounds to P.O.P. to fight this

election? Yes, and we also know that the Americans have
been ever more generous, although we don't have the
figures as yet. (p. 142.)

So says Nanga to Odili whom he tries to discourage first by laugh-
ing at him, then offering him a scholarship to study overseas.
Nanga does this because, he says, 'I feel after all my years of
service to my people I deserve to be elected unopposed so my de-
tractors in Bori will know that I have the people solidly behind
me.' (p. 132.) When this fails Nanga places pressure on both
Odili's father, to this point one of his party organizers, and on the
people of Odili's village, by cancelling a project to give the village
pipe-borne water, in order to secure their votes. And when all this
fails to discourage Odili he is given a merciless beating by Nanga's
thugs – in public.

Perhaps the fear of popular rejection accounts for the violence with
which Nanga and his colleagues fight the political campaign. But
Achebe makes plain that rejection will never come from this quarter:

> Some political commentators have said that it was the
> supreme cynicism of these transactions that inflamed the
> people and brought down the Government. That is sheer
> poppycock. The people themselves, as we have seen, had be-
> come even more cynical than their leaders and were apa-
> thetic into the bargain. 'Let them eat,' was the people's
> opinion, 'after all when white men used to do all the eating did
> we commit suicide?' Of course not. And where is the all-
> powerful white man today? He came, he ate and he went. But
> we are still around. The important thing then is to stay alive;
> if you do you will outlive your present annoyance. The great
> thing, as the old people have told us, is reminiscence; and only
> those who survive can have it. Besides, if you survive, who
> knows? It may be your turn to eat tomorrow. Your son may
> bring home your share.
> No, the *people* had nothing to do with the fall of our
> Government. What happened was simply that unruly mobs
> and private armies having tasted blood and power during the
> election had got out of hand and ruined their masters and
> employers. And they had *no public reason* whatever for doing
> it. Let's make no mistake about that. (pp. 161–2. Italics mine.)

And this estimate is confirmed towards the close of the book. Max is killed on election day by Chief Koko's thugs. Koko in turn is killed by Eunice, Max's fiancée. Nothing is changed in the country as a result of the election which is rigged, and Nanga, Koko, and the others are returned.

Meanwhile the Prime Minister had appointed Chief Nanga and the rest of the old Cabinet back to office and announced over the radio that he intended to govern and stamp out subversion and thuggery without quarter or mercy. He assured foreign investors that their money was safe in the country, that his government stood 'as firm as the Rock of Gibraltar' by its open-door economic policy. (p. 161.)

But ironically, Max achieves in death what he would not likely have achieved in living. 'The fighting which broke out that night between Max's bodyguard and Chief Koko's thugs . . . struck a match and lit the tinder of discontent in the land.' (p. 160.) The chaos which follows is subdued by the army which 'obliged us by staging a coup at that point and locking up every member of Government'. (p. 165.) Then, and only then, does the 'body politic' express a concern over the national situation in which until this time they had existed contentedly.

Overnight everyone began to shake their heads at the excesses of the last régime, at its graft, oppression and corrupt government: newspapers, the radio, the hitherto silent intellectuals and civil servants – everybody said what a terrible lot; and it became public opinion the next morning. And these were the same people that only the other day had owned a thousand names of adulation, whom praise-singers followed with song and talking-drum wherever they went. Chief Koko in particular became a thief and a murderer, while the people who had led him on – in my opinion the real culprits – took the legendary bath of the Hornbill and donned innocence. (p. 166.)

The novel's close, so far as the political theme is concerned, offers a rational for postponement. Problems have been identified and brought to the attention not only of the people but of the world. A moment of clarification has taken place and the scene set

E

for a new beginning. But the novel offers no prediction or indication of what this beginning might comprise or where it might lead.
Achebe writes: 'the military régime . . . abolished all political
parties in the country and announced they would remain abolished
"until the situation became stabilised once again".' Achebe has
taken his theme here as far as he intended – he has observed the
limits he set for himself. He has brought the story, initiated in
Things Fall Apart, up to date, at least to the date the book was
published.

The novel is a carefully plotted and unified piece of writing.
Achebe achieves balance and proportion in the treatment of his
theme of political corruption by evoking both the absurdity of the
behaviour of the principal characters while at the same time suggesting the serious and destructive consequences of their behaviour
to the commonwealth. Of the principal characters Odili, Nanga
and Odili's father are the most successful and for different reasons.
Odili's motifs are never entirely disinterested: capable of idealism,
he nevertheless acts often out of self-interest and spitefulness in
his dealings with his protagonist Nanga. He is thus not a stereo-
typed character of a familiar type in novels which treat this subject.

Nanga is, in many ways, a compelling creation. In Achebe's
words:

Chief Nanga was a born politician; he could get away with
almost anything he said or did. And as long as men are swayed
by their hearts and stomachs and not their heads the Chief
Nangas of this world will continue to get away with anything.
He had that rare gift of making people feel – even while he
was saying harsh things to them – that there was not a drop of
ill will in his entire frame. I remember the day he was telling
his ministerial colleague over the telephone in my presence
that he distrusted our young university people and that he
would rather work with a European. I knew I was hearing terrible things but somehow I couldn't bring myself to take the
man seriously. He had been so open and kind to me and not
in the least distrustful. The greatest criticism a man like him
seemed capable of evoking in our country was an indulgent:
'Make you no min' am.'

This is of course a formidable weapon which is always

guaranteed to save its wielder from the normal consequences of misconduct as well as from the humiliation and embarrassment of ignorance. For how else could you account for the fact that a Minister of Culture announced in public that he had never heard of his country's most famous novel and received applause – as indeed he received again later when he prophesied that before long our great country would produce great writers like Shakespeare, Dickens, Jane Austen, Bernard Shaw and – raising his eyes off the script – Michael West and Dudley Stamp. (p. 73.)

The character of Odili's father is presented both as a type and an individual, one who embodies suggestions so typical of the generality of Nigerians of his generation, yet capable of independent and noble action. Describing the father's reactions to his entry into the political campaign, Odili says:

My father's attitude to my political activity intrigued me a lot. He was, as I think I have already indicated, the local chairman of P.O.P. in our village, Urua, and so I expected that his house would not contain both of us. But I was quite wrong. He took the view (without expressing it in so many words) that the main-spring of political action was personal gain, a view which, I might say, was much more in line with the general feeling in the country than the high-minded thinking of fellows like Max and I. The only comment I remember my father making (at the beginning anyway) was when he asked if my 'new' party was ready to give me enough money to fight Nanga. He sounded a little doubtful. But he was clearly satisfied with what I had got out of it so far, especially the car which he was now using nearly as much as myself. The normal hostility between us was put away in a corner, out of sight. But very soon all that was to change, and then change again. (p. 128.)

The father is the local chairman of Nanga's party but reconciles the apparent contradiction implied by his generous welcome of Odili's friends by citing a proverb which says: 'I believe that the hawk should perch and the eagle perch, whichever says to the other *don't*, may it break its own wing.' (p. 138.) The father is made to suffer for standing by his son and in doing so, not only is a

reconciliation possible, but a nobility of character and attitude
which transcends the local and immediate situation is suggested:

> When I came back with my newspapers the next day I was told
> that Councillor 'Couple' had come to see my father with a
> promise that if he signed a certain document his recent tax
> levy would be refunded to him. The document merely sought
> to dissociate him from his son's lunatic activities; it also said
> that the so-called launching of C.P.C. in his premises was
> done without his knowledge and consent and concluded by
> affirming his implicit confidence in our great and God-fearing
> leader, Chief Nanga.
>
> I could visualize my father reading it carefully with his now
> rarely used spectacles and then, putting his glasses aside, tell-
> ing the fellow to carry his corpse off. And he must have run –
> so much so that he left the document behind. 'You made a
> serious mistake today,' I told my father later that day. 'In
> your eyes have I ever done anything else in all my life?'
>
> 'I am talking about this paper you refused to sign.' He was
> silent for a while, then he said: 'You may be right. But our
> people have said that a man of worth never gets up to unsay
> what he said yesterday. I received your friends in my house
> and I am not going to deny it.' (p. 152.)

As in the earlier novels, Achebe's use of English is appropriate
to his theme. In *A Man of the People* he makes considerable use
of 'pidgin English', the *lingua franca* of West Africa. Used generally as a language of a kind of comic expression *pidgin* has, as
Achebe reveals, a close correlation to the sentiments of the common
man and can be used to reflect serious as well as comic considerations. Take, for example, this exchange between Odili and some of
his campaign workers:

> One early morning Boniface and one of the other stalwarts
> woke me up and demanded twenty-five pounds. I knew that a
> certain amount of exploitation was inevitable in this business
> and I wasn't going to question how every penny was spent. But
> at the same time I didn't see how I could abdicate my respon-
> sibility for C.P.C. funds entrusted to me. I had to satisfy
> my conscience that I was exercising adequate control.

'I gave you ten pounds only yesterday,' I said and was about to add that unlike our opponents we had very limited funds – a point which I had already made many times. But Boniface interrupted me.

'Are you there?' he said. 'If na play we de play make you tell us because me I no wan waste my time for nothing sake. Or you think say na so so talk talk you go take win Chief Nanga. If Government no give you plenty money for election make you go tell them no be sand sand we de take do am. . . .'

'Man no fit fight tiger with empty hand,' added his companion before I could put in a word to correct Boniface's fantastic misconception.

'No be Government de give us money,' I said. 'We na small party, C.P.C. We wan help poor people like you. How Government go give us money . . . ?'

'But na who de give the er weting call . . . P.C.P. money?' asked Boniface puzzled.

'Some friends abroad,' I said with a knowing air to cover my own ignorance which I had forgotten to worry about in the heat of activity.

'You no fit send your friends telegram?' asked Boniface's companion.

'Let's not go into that now. What do you need twenty-five pounds for? And what have you done with the ten pounds?' (pp. 126–7.)

A Man of the People attracted considerable attention when it was published because the military take-over described in the closing passages coincided with the military take-over in Nigeria in January, 1966, the month of the novel's publication. The novel had, and still has, topicality. There is no necessary correlation between topicality and art: often a novel achieves the status of art when it transcends the local and the particular. The closing paragraph of the book suggests a generalization about human experience which the events of the novel have dramatized, however local these events have been. Early in the novel Josiah, a local trader, a supporter of Nanga's party in Odili's village, is driven from the village for stealing. Josiah returns at the time of the election, a powerful influence with Nanga's support. When the military

coup takes place and political parties arc abolished, the members of
the former party are wholly discredited, among them Chiefs
Nanga and Koko.

The closing paragraphs of the novel reveal Achebe's assessment
of the specific circumstances the novel dramatizes while at the
same time suggesting the appropriateness of such an assessment to
any situation where similar conditions obtain. The terms of reference are local, the application general. The irony is of a familiar
kind:

> 'Koko had taken enough for the owner to see,' said my
> father to me. It was the day I had gone to visit Eunice and
> was telling him on my return how the girl had showed no
> interest in anything – including whether she stayed in jail or
> out of it. My father's words struck me because they were the
> very same words the villagers of Anata had spoken of Josiah,
> the abominated trader. Only in their case the words had mean-
> ing. The owner was the village, and the village had a mind; it
> could say no to sacrilege. But in the affairs of the nation there
> was no owner, the laws of the village became powerless. Max
> was avenged not by the people's collective will but by one soli-
> tary woman who loved him. Had his spirit waited for the
> people to demand redress it would have been waiting still, in
> the rain and out in the sun. But he was lucky. And I don't
> mean it to shock or to sound clever. For I do honestly believe
> that in the fat-dripping, gummy, eat-and-let-eat régime just
> ended – a régime which inspired the common saying that a
> man could only be sure of what he had put away safely in his
> gut or, in language ever more suited to the times: 'you chop,
> me self I chop, palavcr finish'; a régime in which you saw a
> fellow cursed in the morning for stealing a blind man's stick
> and later in the evening saw him again mounting the altar
> of the new shrine in the presence of all the people to whisper
> into the ear of the chief celebrant – in such a régime, I say,
> you died a good death if your life had inspired someone to
> come forward and shoot your murderer in the chest – without
> asking to be paid. (pp. 166–7.)

Conclusion

▼▼▼▼▼▼▼▼▼▼▼▼▼▼▼▼▼▼▼▼▼▼▼▼▼▼▼▼▼▼▼

A MAN OF THE PEOPLE while different in tone, more immediate in subject and more deliberately polemical in purpose than any of the other novels, completes a sequence of novels which reveal the changes wrought in Nigerian life during the twentieth century, the period beginning with the *Pacification of the Primitive Tribes of the Lower Niger* and ending in the post-independence setting. This tetrology of novels reveals the extent to which traditional values have been turned upside down and ends in gloom and uncertainty. Achebe chooses his examples from 'the Nigerian society I know best – Ibo society'. But analogies with other ethnic groups are probably apparent to readers from those groups. And to overseas readers the overall implications of the major themes of the novels and their implied conclusions will be obvious.

The novels reveal much more than a study of the traumatic effects of colonialism on a subject people even though this is a serious part of their intention. Achebe recognizes his obligation to his society and has said of himself that he must participate in the task of 're-education and re-generation' which must be done. This places him in a quite different relation to his society than writers in Europe and America. He lives in his society and expresses its aspirations; they appear by and large, in revolt against their societies. Modern African writers speak primarily for and to the peoples of their own countries – express their hopes and fears, sum up their experiences and establish (or re-establish) the uniqueness and dignity of their communities. As well, as has been noted, these writers bring news of strange parts of the world to the generality of overseas readers and as such serve the same function. Modern African writing, like all literature, has a special commitment to formulating the basic values of society and is both a reflection and a criticism of those values. It creates a sensation of the life of the society and as such forms part of the total cultural accretion of the society. Achebe recognizes the educative role of the writer when he says of him that he is 'the sensitive point in the community'. The writer is especially equipped to know in a sensitive way what is prominent in the minds, what are the most pressing concerns of the people of and for whom he writes. He has the responsibility of synthesizing these values and interpreting them. The educative role of the writer which Achebe accepts involves him in the formulation of the social and cultural philosophy and values of society which he casts in the most effective and convincing form that he can command. Part of Achebe's concern has been with reconciling the individual with his cultural heritage on the one hand, and his culture in a time of crisis on the other. His task then has been not only to show through the life he creates and evokes in his novels that African life before the coming of the white man was 'not one long night of savagery' but to assert the rights and obligations which are conferred on the generality of people in contemporary society. The past informs the present as Achebe implies when he writes: 'The writer's duty is not to beat this morning's headlines in topicality, it is to explore the depth of the human condition. In Africa he cannot perform this task unless he has a proper sense of history.' He says further:

> I believe that the writer should be concerned with the question of human values. One of the most distressing ills which afflict new nations is a confusion of values. We sometimes make the mistake of talking about values as though they were fixed and eternal. . . . Of course values are relative and in a constant state of flux.[26]

The writer, according to this helps to establish values and often assists a generality of people in making a single choice from the many choices open to them. Ultimately in this respect, Achebe's quest has been to find in the aspirations of his contemporary society new ways of reaching understanding in the light of traditional values as they are confronted with the impact of modern ideas.

The published short stories, not many more in number than the

novels, reveal the same interests as the longer fiction. They are
found in Black Orpheus and in a volume entitled *The Sacrificial
Egg and other Stories*.* They fall into two classes: those which
show an aspect of the conflict between traditional and modern
values – for example, 'The Sacrificial Egg,' 'Dead Man's Path'
and 'Beginning of the End' – and those which display the nature
of custom or religious belief without attempting to probe or explain their meanings. In fact, such a separation is arbitrary: in the
best stories the conflict between the traditional and the modern
has its base in the general religious beliefs which inform the former.

'Dead Man's Path' (published first in 1953) tells the story of
Michael Obi, a young teacher, who sees in his appointment as
headmaster to a mission school the chance to introduce modern
ideas. Obi's ideas of 'modernity' are fairly superficial and consist
in part of tidying up the school yard and arranging it after the
manner of European gardens. In doing this he plants across a
pathway which leads to a traditional burial ground and when the
villagers continue to use the path he plants it more densely and
strengthens it with barbed wire. The village priest pays him a
visit and tells him that the path must be left open for the use of the
villagers. For both Obi and the priest the path is a symbol. For
the priest it represents the continuity of life and religion: 'The
whole life of the village depends upon it and our ancestors visit
us by it. But more important our unborn babes cannot arrive
any other way.' (p. 15.) For Michael Obi it is a symbol of attitudes,
out of date, which have no place in the modern world: 'The whole
purpose of our school . . . is to show the folly of such beliefs as
you now hold. Dead men do not require footpaths. The whole
idea is just fantastic.' (p. 15.)

But tradition here is inflexible. 'What you say may be true . . .
but we will follow the practise of our fathers. If you re-open the
path we will have nothing to quarrel about,' says the priest. But
Michael Obi does not reopen the path and when a few days later
a baby dies Obi 'woke up . . . among the ruins of his work. The
beautiful hedges were torn up and the flowers trampled to death. . .'
Ironically, 'a few days later, the Government Supervisor came to
inspect the school,' and Obi may be judged to have failed since the

* Achebe, Chinua, *The Sacrificial Egg and Other Stories*, Etudo Limited,
Onitsha, 1962. All page references to this edition.

school stands for the modern and the forces of conservatism have prevailed.

Achebe is impartial here: neither side is supported. Obi, despite his somewhat frivolous attitude and the seeming paucity of his idealism, is never allowed to explain himself. Nor, on the other hand, does the priest question the validity of the religion he expounds. The force of the story lies in its suggestiveness rather than any explicit statement it makes.

The same is so with 'Beginning of the End'. Here Nnaemeka, a young Iboman living in Lagos, falls in love with an Ibibio girl, Neneataga. He seeks to win his father's support for his marriage but when this is not forthcoming marries the girl anyway. The marriage is a happy one marred only by the old man's refusal over eight long years to speak about his son. (There are superficial similarities between the situation here and that of Obi and Clara in *No Longer at Ease*.) Finally his daughter-in-law writes to him:

'. . . . Our two sons, from the day they learnt that they have a grandfather, have insisted on being taken to him. I find it impossible to tell them that you will not see them. I implore you to allow Nnaemeka to bring them home for a short time during his leave next month. I shall remain here in Lagos. . . .'

The old man at once felt the resolution he had built up over so many years falling in. He was telling himself that he must not give in. He tried to steel his heart against all emotional appeals. The internal conflict was terrible. He leaned against a window and looked out. It was one of those rare occasions when even Nature takes a hand in a human fight. The sky was overcast with heavy black clouds. Very soon it began to rain – the first rain in the year. It came down in large sharp drops and was accompanied by the lightning and thunder which mark a change of season. Okeke was trying hard not to think of his grandchildren. But he knew he was fighting a losing battle. He tried to hum a favourite hymn tune but the pattering of large drops on the roof supplied a harsh accompaniment. He gave it up and was immediately thinking of the children. How could he shut his door against them? By a curious mental process he imagined them standing, sad and forsaken, under the harsh angry weather – shut out from his house.

That night he hardly slept, from remorse. (p. 26.)

Here a happy resolution is attained and modern values win out, a significant albeit a small triumph, and conservatism is defeated.

The Sacrificial Egg offers yet another view of the conflict between the generations and the beliefs held by each. This is a superb example of short story writing for in some fifteen hundred words Achebe is able to suggest a locale where traditional practices in terms of belief and daily commerce are maintained yet intensified by contact with Europe, and to suggest the moment at which a young Iboman 'whose education placed him above such superstitious stuff' as belief in the presence of members of the spirit world in the world of the living, through a moment of intense violence and pain is forced to re-examine his beliefs.

The time is 1920 and Julius Obi comes from his bush village to work as a clerk for the Niger Company at a port on the Niger. He falls in love with Janet whose mother, called Ma, although a Christian fills him with local lore about spirits. A smallpox epidemic strikes the town and Julius is told not to see Janet until the epidemic is over. On his last visit to her they said good night and shook hands 'which was very odd'. On his way home Julius steps on a 'sacrificial egg and crushes it. He had crushed it and taken the sufferer's ill luck to himself.' His sceptical mind rejects the traditional idea as nonsense and he presses on home.

> But it was too late; the night spirit was already abroad. Its voice rose high and clear in the still, black air. It was a long way away, but Julius knew that distance did not apply to these beings. So he made straight for the cocoyam farm beside the road and threw himself on his belly. He had hardly done this when he heard the rattling staff of the spirit and thundering stream of esoteric speech. He shook all over. The sounds came bearing down on him. And then he could hear the footsteps. It was as if twenty men were running together. In no time at all the sounds had passed and disappeared in the distance on the other side of the road. (p. 11.)

The sacrificial egg, it is implied, serves the purpose for which it was intended. Julius is forced to take on the misfortunes of someone else. Janet and her mother are carried away by the smallpox. Nothing is explained since belief of a religious kind is anti-pathetic to rational scrutiny. The mystery remains a mystery. But the psychological consequences of the events are left behind and promote feelings of desolation and loss.

'Akeuke', the last story in the volume, communicates the same sense of mystery and the same preference for suggesting rather than explaining meaning. 'Akeuke' tells of a young woman, the youngest member of a family and the only girl, who contracts a disease which causes her abdomen to swell. It tells of her brothers' concern for her, their sympathy with her illness on the one hand, and their fear of communal reprisal for allowing a woman with an abominated disease to remain in the village.

> . . . Akeuke had been stricken with the swelling disease which was an abomination to *Ani*, the earth. The victim must on no account be permitted to die in the house, but must be taken to the bad bush and left there to die alone. Akeuke knew the purpose of her brothers' consultation. As soon as the eldest set foot in her sick room she began to scream at him, and he fled. This went on for a whole day, and there was a real danger that she might die in the house and bring down the anger of *Ani* on the whole family, if not the entire village. Neighbours came in and warned the brothers of the grave danger to which they were exposing the nine villages of Umuofia. (p. 30.)

Eventually she is cast into the 'bad bush' and when her brothers return the next day she has disappeared, thought by them to have been carried away by an animal. After three months their grandfather summons them before him. Having had their assurance that Akeuke is dead:

> The old man gnashed his teeth, and then rose painfully three-quarters erect and tottered towards his sleeping room, moved back the carved door and the ghost of Akeuke stood before them, unsmiling and implacable. Everyone sprang to his feet and one or two were already outside. (p. 31.)

That is all there is to the story. Nothing is explained – the mystery remains. Michael Echeruo comments on these stories 'Achebe writes these two stories as if he believed them, without the "superior" pose which very often mars fiction of that kind' and goes on to offer a prediction:

If it is in the direction of stories like 'Akeuke' and 'The Sacrificial Egg' that Achebe plans to move in his future fiction, and if he can sustain that independent sympathy, this 'credulousness' which rightly belongs – or used to belong – to the folktale, he would have chosen a form which could enable him to bridge the gulf between the innocence of Amos Tutuola and Ekwensi's sophistication. (p. 6.)

To join for a moment in what is largely a futile exercise, it seems safe to suppose that recent events in Nigeria will determine the direction in which Achebe will move when the next novels are written. It is inconceivable that a writer who has defined and exploited the role of novelist in the way Achebe has to date, could or would stand aside from treating events which have shaken so badly, if not destroyed, the federation which held out such 'wonderful prospects'. In the same article from which that quotation is taken Achebe says 'the reality of present-day Africa [sic: 1966] . . . may change as a result of deliberate, e.g. political action. If it does an entirely new situation will arise, and there will be plenty of time to examine it.'[27] That time has come and Achebe has indicated the relevance of the change to himself as writer; when he says: 'It is clear to me that an African creative writer who tries to avoid the big social and political issues of contemporary Africa will end up being completely irrelevant – like that absurd man in the proverb who leaves his burning house to pursue a rat fleeing from the flames.'[28]

The historical, political, social background in its complexity is important to Achebe; his theme is history in an important sense. Equally important is his interest in exploring the depths of the human condition. His concern therefore is with individuals whose passions and hopes and fears are permanent in mankind. Abiola Irele sums up as well as can be the relevance of Achebe's writing:

> . . . a novelist deals not only with situations but also, and above all, with individuals. And it is precisely the cycle created by the responses of men to the pressure of events, their evolutions at significant levels of feeling and thought, that makes the real world of the novel. The importance of Chinua Achebe's novels derives not simply from his theme, but also from his complete presentation of men in action, in living

reaction to their fate, as well as from his own perception that underlies his imaginative world and confers upon it relevance and truth.[29]

Achebe's novels offer a vision of life which is essentially tragic, compounded of success and failure, informed by knowledge and understanding, relieved by humour and tempered by sympathy, embued with an awareness of human suffering and the human capacity to endure. Sometimes his characters meet with success, more often with defeat and despair. Through it all the spirit of man and the belief in the possibility of triumph endures.

Notes

▼▼▼▼▼▼▼▼▼▼▼▼▼▼▼▼▼▼▼▼▼▼▼▼▼▼▼▼▼▼▼▼▼▼▼▼▼

Introduction
1. Heywood, Christopher 'Surface and Symbol in *Things Fall Apart*' *Journal of the Nigerian English Studies Association* No 2 Ibadan Nov. 1967 pp. 41–45
2. Achebe, Chinua 'The English Language and the African Writer' *Insight* Oct/Dec. 1966, pp. 19–20
3. Serumaga, Robert 'Interview with Chinua Achebe' Transcription Centre, London 1967 p. 1
4. Achebe, Chinua 'The Black Writer's Burden' *Presence Africaine* Paris 1962 p. 135
5. Achebe 'The English Language and the African Writer' p. 20
6. 'The Black Writer's Burden' p. 135
7. 'The English Language and the African Writer' p. 20
8. 'The English Language and the African Writer' p. 21
9. 'The Role of the Writer in a New Nation' *Nigeria Magazine* No. 81 June 1964 p. 160
10. 'The Novelist as Teacher' *New Statesman* 29 January 1965 p. 162
11. 'The Role of the Writer in a New Nation' p. 158
12. 'The Novelist as Teacher' p. 162
13. Serumaga 'Interview with Chinua Achebe' p. 1
14. Achebe 'The Role of the Writer in a New Nation' p. 158
15. 'The Role of the Writer in a New Nation' p. 158
16. 'The Role of the Writer in a New Nation' p. 160

Things Fall Apart
17. Achebe 'The Role of the Writer in a New Nation' p. 158
18. Irele, Abiola 'The Tragic Conflict in Achebe's Novels' *Introduction to African Literature* (ed. Beier) Longmans 1967 p. 170
19. Achebe 'The Role of the Writer in a New Nation' p. 179

Arrow of God
20. Achebe 'Interview with Lewis Nkosi' *Africa Report* July 1964 p. 20

21. 'Interview with Lewis Nkosi' p. 21
22. Serumaga 'Interview with Chinua Achebe' p. 3

A Man of the People
23. Serumaga 'Interview with Chinua Achebe' p. 11
24. Consider the behaviour of the masked figures in, for example, *Things Fall Apart*, when Okonkwo's compound is levelled by Masked Spirits for the sin he has committed in killing a kinsman.
25. Achebe 'The Role of the Writer in a New Nation' p. 159

Conclusion
26. Achebe 'The Role of the Writer in a New Nation' p. 159
27. 'The English Language and the African Writer' p. 19
28. '*Biafra Lifeline*' New York 1968 p. 1
29. Irele, Abiola 'The Tragic Conflict in Achebe's Novels' p. 32